D0784558

MEMORABLE MEALS IN MINUTES

Rosamond Richardson is the author of several cookery books, and the presenter of the BBC TV series 'Discovering Patchwork' and 'Discovering Hedgerows'. She lives in Castle Hedingham, Essex with her husband and three children. An experienced cook but also a very busy mother, she knows the joy of being able to prepare delicious and imaginative meals quickly and easily. Her book contains a wealth of varied recipes: rapid appetisers, snappy soups, nimble fish dishes, dizzy desserts, and many more. No busy cook should be without it.

Memorable Meals in Minutes

Rosamond Richardson

Illustrated by Hilary Wills

CORONET BOOKS
Hodder and Stoughton

Copyright © 1983 Rosamond Richardson

First published in Great Britain 1983
by Coronet Books

British Library C.I.P.

Richardson, Rosamond
  Memorable meals in minutes.
  1 Cookery
  I Title
  641.5'55   TX652

ISBN 0-340-33206-9

Printed and bound in Great Britain for
Hodder and Stoughton Paperbacks, a
division of Hodder and Stoughton Ltd.,
Mill Road, Dunton Green, Sevenoaks,
Kent (Editorial Office: 47 Bedford
Square, London, WC1 3DP) by Collins, Glasgow.

For Nicholas, in memory of Monday afternoons in Cambridge

CONTENTS

INTRODUCTION

The philosophy behind this book could perhaps be summed up as elegance with ease. Most people love good food, and who does not enjoy a memorable meal? But equally, although you may like cooking, you don't necessarily like feeling exhausted at the end of the process. I have given so many dinner parties which seemed to take days to prepare and at least a day to clear up afterwards, and I've thought to myself 'Never again! It's not worth it' – even though the party itself has been great fun. And when it comes to the daily round of cooking, the same principle applies: who would not wish to produce and eat elegant dishes with the minimum of drudgery?

So I have developed a style of cooking which means spending the shortest possible time in the kitchen, and a way of stocking the house that finds most things easily to hand. I find it so refreshing to know that I need spend no more than half an hour at the stove before producing a delicious meal of two or three courses, with no sense of panic or rush. This way of cooking is fun because it is light and beautifully simple, and the results are mouth-wateringly delicious. It means that your daily fare can be effortlessly varied without having to spend hours working in the kitchen, and when it comes to dinner parties, it liberates you to enjoy a special occasion without feeling worn out. And then of course there are times when perhaps you get back later than you had planned, or someone arrives out of the blue: with no special shopping, no planning ahead, and no mopping of the brow, you can make an effortless and elegant meal in a matter of minutes.

There are several hints to help you make this dream-like philosophy come true. Stock up your larder and freezer, if you have one, with the lists on pages 13-14, and you will cut down immensely on incidental shopping time. Organise your kitchen as described on page 11, and arm yourself with good tools (see pages 11-12).

Remember that you can always start a meal with something from your local delicatessen, or, for example, keep a whole salami hanging in the larder: so long as it is cool it will keep for several months. When it comes to a third course, many people are just as happy with fresh fruit as with a dessert, either with or instead of a cheese board.

All the recipes in this book take a matter of minutes to prepare, and whilst the dishes are cooking you can either prepare another course, or leave the kitchen to enjoy the company of family or friends. It is the best way to enjoy good food in your own home, and to be free from feeling like a slave is a luxury. There is another advantage, too, which is that both family and friends prefer an unruffled cook and hostess. You can revolutionise the image of fine food with this approach and finish up with a new way of life spent mostly out of the kitchen and yet heightened by memorable meals.

Rosamond Richardson

TIPS AND TOOLS

A good workman never blames his tools, they say. So make sure you've got good ones – there is no doubt that first-class equipment helps you to be a first-class cook. Cooking is a craft and all crafts require specific tools. So arm yourself with excellent artillery before you go into battle.

I rely heavily on my liquidiser, and would not be without my electric beater. On the wall over my working surface I have some wall-scales which I swear by: they are out of the way while I am working but always ready for use. Next to that is my magnetic knife rack with a wonderful selection of good knives – steel, stainless steel, serrated, curved – you name it, they're all there. I have a wall tin-opener which saves me a great deal of frustration, and a set of metal spoon-measures which hang on the wall next to the knives. Herbs and spices are lined up on a rack on the wall in opaque jars so that the light does not spoil them, and in a cupboard above the working surface live a measuring cup and measuring jugs, fruit juicer, mandoline slicer, cheese slicer, cheese grater and egg beater. I keep my army of wooden spoons, sieves, rubber scrapers and the ever-in-use garlic press in a pretty basket on the side, and have left a space for a food-processor that I have been promised for Christmas!

If you organise your kitchen so that you have to walk a minimum of miles to find the tools that you need, your life will be made far more pleasant. I even got an extension lead put on to the kitchen phone so that I didn't have to watch helplessly as the milk boiled over in the middle of a vital conversation. Now I can chat as I pull things out of the oven or stir a sauce on the stove. I use as much oven-to-table ware as possible, and the best thing I ever bought was a pair of ceramic colanders: I just drain vegetables in them – which of course instantly heats the dish – and put them on their matching plates on the table. Various gadgets certainly make life in the kitchen

11

easier, too, and everyone has their favourite. First on my list is the dishwasher, and second – from the sublime to the ridiculous – a Scandinavian cheese slicer which pares slender, transparent slices off a block of cheese.

Having organised your kitchen so that you can work in it with ease, stock your larder and freezer with the items suggested on page 13 and 14, and you will find that you can make all the recipes in this book with no extra shopping. If you are well-stocked it will save you nipping out to the corner shop because you have run out of butter or bacon. Another way to cut down on shopping time is to plan menus in advance and buy everything in one go. You can economise on time by using frozen vegetables, although don't waste your time with ones that freeze badly. Spinach, broad beans, carrots, sweetcorn and broccoli all freeze admirably. Frozen sugar peas and tomatoes make good soups, but both French and runner beans are best straight out of the garden or the shopping basket. Another way of cutting down on time is to use vegetables that need very little in the way of washing and peeling. Avocado, French beans, sweetcorn, tomatoes, peppers, leeks, mushrooms, cauliflower, cabbage, cucumber and courgettes are all such vegetables.

Finally, I am a great believer in making both the food and the table look pretty. I love houseplants and so there is usually something in flower that I can put on the table; in the early summer I pick bunches of herbs in flower, or a bunch of wild flowers and grasses from the garden. I keep a store of candles in all sorts of colours because candlelight always adds glamour to a meal. I also have a selection of pretty paper napkins so that I can decorate the table with the colour of my mood. Make it all look lovely, and everyone will enjoy their memorable meals all the more.

A SHOPPING LIST FOR YOUR LARDER SHELVES

olive oil
walnut or groundnut oil
white wine vinegar
mayonnaise
Dijon mustard
jif-lemon
tomato purée
curry paste
soy sauce
green peppercorns
olives
a string of garlic
salami on a string
sesame seeds
almonds
walnuts
macaroons
cooking chocolate

ginger in syrup
tinned peaches
cooking brandy
Kirsch
tins of:
  rollmop herrings
  anchovy fillets
  lumpfish roe
  smoked oysters
  consommé
  pimentoes
  tomatoes
  tuna fish
  snails
  beansprouts
  water chestnuts
  baby sweetcorn
  sweetcorn (off the cob)

A SHOPPING LIST FOR YOUR FREEZER

Fish
smoked mackerel
smokies
kipper fillets
mussels
scallops
crabmeat
sole and plaice

Meat
chicken livers
kidneys
lamb's liver
sausages
bacon
chicken pieces
turkey breasts
veal escalopes
rabbit joints

Vegetables
sugar peas
tomatoes
spinach
peas
broad beans
corn on the cob

Fruit
apples
pears
raspberries

ice creams
sorbets
butter
pastry (both puff and shortcrust),
vol- au-vent cases

CONVERSION TABLES

WEIGHTS

½ oz	10 g (grams)
1	25
1½	40
2	50
2½	60
3	75
4	100
4½	125
5	150
6	175
7	200
8	225
9	250
10	275
12	350
1 lb	450
1½	700
2	900
3	1 kg 350 g

VOLUME

2 fl oz	55 ml
3 fl oz	75
5 fl oz (¼ pint)	150
½ pint	275
¾ pint	425
1 pint	570
1¾ pints	1 litre
(2-pint basin – 1 litre)	

TEMPERATURES

Mark		
1	275°F	140°C
2	300	150
3	325	170
4	350	180
5	375	190
6	400	200
7	425	210
8	450	220

MEASUREMENTS

⅛ in	3 mm (millimetre)
¼ in	½ cm (centimetre)
½	1
¾	2
1	2.5
1¼	3
1½	4
1¾	4.5
2	5
3	7.5
4	10
5	13
6	15
7	18
8	20
9	23
10	25.5
11	28
12	30

Salted Almonds
Anchoiade
Scandi-anchies
Anchovy Rollers
Anchovy Spread
Potted Tongue
Canadian Snackers
Parsley Squares
Smoked Mackerel Goodies
Deep-fried Shrimps
Vol-au-Vent Specials
Chicken Liver Vol-au-Vents
Very Light Chicken Liver Pâté
Rollmop Delight
Special Melon
Luxury Avocado
Guacamole
Linda's Avocado Pâté
French Celeriac
Quick Cheese Straws
Sesame Sticks

I like to be relaxed about a first course: sometimes it's a shame to disturb a comfortable chat with a summons to table, so often I pass around a plate of nibbles, or even something that is substantial enough to take the place of a first course. These recipes allow for flexibility: some are just nibbles, others are little goodies that you can equally well eat off your lap as serve up as hors d'oeuvres.

Salted Almonds

Delicious with a drink, but beware of their more-ishness!

blanched whole almonds
olive oil
salt

Heat the oil in a frying pan until it is quite hot but not smoking, and toss the almonds in it until they are golden brown: they brown quite quickly so be careful that they do not burn. Drain them on kitchen paper and sprinkle with salt while they are still warm. Leave to cool, and store in airtight jars.

To prepare: 5 minutes

Anchoiade

Serves 4

Serve these little morsels either as a first course garnished with radish-flowers and slices of tomato, or hand them round on their own with drinks before the meal.

1 tin anchovy fillets
1 small bunch of fresh parsley
chopped garlic to taste
oil
4 slices of bread
butter

Rinse the anchovy fillets and cut them up. Pound them to a paste in a mortar. Add the chopped parsley and garlic and oil from the tin plus a little more if necessary.

Cut the crusts off the bread, toast it and cut into squares. Butter the squares, spread with the anchovy mixture, put a knob of butter on to each square and melt it under the grill. Serve immediately.

To prepare: 7 minutes

Scandi-anchies

Serves 4

This combination of anchovy with crunchy dill pickle comes from Scandinavia and is a good palate-freshener.

1 tin anchovy fillets
2 oz/50 g butter, softened
chopped fresh tarragon and chervil
1 large dill pickle
1 tablespoon (15 ml spoon) capers
black pepper
2 large slices of bread

Drain, rinse and chop the anchovy fillets. Mash the butter with a fork and add the anchovies and the chopped herbs, dill pickle and capers. Season with black pepper. Fry the bread and cut into quarters. Heap the anchovy mixture on to the squares and serve with pre-dinner drinks. I sometimes serve it instead of a first course and nobody complains!

To prepare: 10 minutes

Anchovy Rollers

Another anchovy recipe that is useful as a cocktail snack.

Pre-heat oven to gas mark 7/425°F/220°C

Spread thin slices of crustless brown bread with butter, on both sides, and add a smattering of French mustard to taste. Cut into long, narrow fingers, place a rinsed anchovy fillet on each finger and roll up. Secure with a toothpick and cook for 6–8 minutes. Serve at once.

To prepare: 3 minutes
Cooking time: 6–8 minutes

Anchovy Spread

Serves 4

This unusual and delicious paste comes from Magdalen College, Oxford. It was given to my mother by a don's wife when we lived in Cambridge, and I remember it gracing many a college sherry-party!

1 bunch of fresh parsley
2 anchovy fillets
2 oz/50 g butter

Boil the parsley until it is quite soft, about 5 minutes, and drain it. Leave it to cool and then chop it finely. Meanwhile pound the two anchovy fillets in a mortar and mash with the softened butter until thoroughly blended. Add the parsley and mix well. Shape into little balls and serve chilled, either like pâté with dry toast, or on cocktail biscuits as a snack.

To prepare: 10 minutes

Potted Tongue

Serves 4

I love this way of serving tongue, and it is a useful standby since it stores for weeks in the fridge.

4 oz/100 g cooked tongue
4 oz/100 g clarified butter
mace, salt and pepper to season

Chop the tongue finely and melt 3 oz/75 g of the butter. Blend the two together well. Season to taste and pack into a jar. Melt the remaining butter and pour over to seal it. Serve chilled on little squares of toast or fried bread.

To prepare: 5 minutes

Canadian Snackers

Serves 4

One of the best cooks that I have ever had the luck to dine with gave me these 'snackers' as she called them, on a visit to Canada. She generously gave me the recipe and ever since they have been firm favourites with family and friends alike.

3 oz/75 g cream cheese
1 small jar lumpfish roe
half a small onion
lemon juice
pepper

Mash the softened cream cheese and mix in the lumpfish roe thoroughly. Chop the onion very finely and stir in. Add a generous amount of lemon juice and season with pepper.

You can either spread this on to dry cheese biscuits and serve it cold, or make tiny square sandwiches and fry them quickly in hot oil until golden on both sides, which will take about 5–8 minutes. Drain them on kitchen paper and serve immediately on a warm plate.

To prepare: 5 minutes
Cooking time: 5–8 minutes

Parsley Squares

Serves 4

This is a variation on the theme of the Canadian snackers – the poor man's version if you like. In which case, happy are the poor, for these are scrumptious.

8 thin slices of bread
3 oz/75 g garlic and parsley butter (see page 151)
3 oz/75 g Cheddar, sliced paper thin

Pre-heat oven to gas mark 6/400°F/200°C

Butter the bread on both sides and then make sandwiches with the slivers of cheese. Cut into small squares and bake for 20–25 minutes. Serve at once.

To prepare: 5 minutes
Cooking time: 20–25 minutes

Smoked Mackerel Goodies

Serves 4

The softness of the smoked mackerel pâté is a mouthwatering foil to the crisp fried bread squares.

4 slices of bread
6 oz/175 g smoked mackerel
2 oz/50 g softened butter
lemon juice
salt and pepper

Cut the crusts off the bread and cut each slice into four squares. Deep-fry in very hot oil for half a minute until golden all over. Drain on kitchen paper. Mash the smoked mackerel with the butter and season to taste with lemon juice, salt and pepper. Spread on to the cooled fried bread squares and serve.

To prepare: 8 minutes

Deep-fried Shrimps

I first had these in the heart of Greece under a blistering midday sun looking out to sea in a tiny village. We watched the fishermen pulling in their nets full of tiny shrimps, and a matter of minutes later they were served up on hot plates in front of us. We unashamedly ate a second helping.

Instead of laboriously having to peel the tiny creatures you can cook them whole, and they are delicious: use either the minute brown shrimps or the slightly larger pink variety – they both work very well. They should be as fresh as possible.

Just heat a pan of deep cooking oil to chip heat and fry the shrimps until they are crisp, which will take two or three minutes. Drain them on kitchen paper and serve hot, with wedges of lemon.

To prepare: 5 minutes

Vol-au-Vent Specials

Serves 4

These are a real treat: effortless and epicurean.

12 small vol-au-vent cases
1 tin smoked oysters
¼ pint/150 ml béchamel sauce
a little cream
salt and pepper

Pre-heat oven to gas mark 5/375°F/190°C

Cook the vol-au-vent cases as instructed on the packet. Cool on a
rack.

Chop the smoked oysters very finely and add to the béchamel
sauce with a little of the juice from the tin. Finish with a little cream
and season to taste. Fill the vol-au-vent cases with the mixture, and
heat through for 8-10 minutes until sizzling hot, and serve.

To prepare: 8 minutes
Cooking time: 8 – 10 minutes

Chicken Liver Vol-au-Vents

Serves 4

The softness of this creamy pâté contrasted with crisp light pastry
makes these winners every time.

Fill 12 cooked vol-au-vent cases with Very Light Chicken Liver
Pâté (below). Warm through for a few minutes and serve.

To prepare: 2 minutes
Cooking time: 5 minutes

Very Light Chicken Liver Pâté

Serves 4-6

1 large Spanish onion
6 oz/175 g butter
8 oz/225 g chicken livers
salt and pepper

Slice the onion very finely and sweat it in 2 oz/50 g of the butter until very soft, covered and over a low heat. It will take about 10 minutes. Meanwhile melt another 2 oz/50 g butter and sauté the chicken livers quickly until done on the outside but still pink inside. Put in the blender with the remaining butter, melted. Add the onion mixture, a little salt and generous amounts of pepper, and liquidise. Leave to cool.

The addition of a little cream and some chopped herbs is delicious, especially if you can lay your hands on fresh basil and thyme.

You can either fill 12 vol-au-vent cases with the pâté and warm through as above, or serve the pâté with fresh toast.

To prepare: 12-15 minutes

Rollmop Delight

Serves 4

Another example of a starter using deep-fried bread – by far the best technique of cooking it; it is crisp right through and as light as a feather.

3 slices of bread
1 small jar of lumpfish roe
2 rollmops
1 hard-boiled egg
fresh parsley

Cut the crusts off the bread and cut into small squares. Deep-fry in very hot oil until they are golden on both sides. Drain on kitchen paper and cool.

Spread the squares with lumpfish roe, put a piece of rollmop herring and a slice of onion from the jar on top. Garnish with a slice of hard-boiled egg and chopped parsley. Serve with pre-dinner drinks.

To prepare: 8 minutes

Special Melon

This recipe comes from the kitchens of a Cambridge college, another dish which reminds me of my childhood in that lovely city. It is a personal favourite of mine, and a wonderful starter for special occasions.

2 honeydew melons
8 oz/225 g peeled prawns
2 oz/50 g butter
curry paste
4 tablespoons (4 x 15 ml spoons) double cream

Cut the melons in half around their waists rather than lengthwise, and remove the pips. Incise the flesh in vertical lines to make it easier to scoop out whilst you are eating it.

Cook the peeled prawns in butter until they are heated through, and add curry paste to taste. Stir in the double cream, heat until piping hot, and put into the half-melons. Serve immediately.

To prepare: 8 minutes

Luxury Avocado

Time for a treat. No cooking involved – about one minute's work to do, and guaranteed contentment.

Wrap chunks of ripe avocado up in strips of Parma ham. Secure them with cocktail sticks and arrange on pretty plates with sesame sticks (see page 29)

To prepare: a few minutes

Guacamole

A famous dish from Mexico. If you can find only unripe avacados, here's a hint from over the Atlantic for how to ripen them overnight: wrap your avocado with a banana in newspaper and it will be soft in 24 hours!

1 large ripe avocado
half a small onion
lemon juice
salt and pepper
6 tablespoons (6 × 15 ml spoons) mayonnaise
1 tablespoon (15 ml spoon) tomato purée
Tabasco

Mash the avocado and mix in the finely chopped or grated onion. Season with generous amounts of lemon juice, add salt and pepper to taste and beat until smooth. Stir in the mayonnaise and the tomato purée until it is the consistency of whipped cream. Season to taste with Tabasco and serve as a dip with crudités and crisps.

To prepare: 5 minutes

Linda's Avocado Pâté

Serves 4

This is simple to make, yet it gives the impression of being highly sophisticated.

1 large ripe avocado
sour cream
chopped fresh parsley
salt and pepper

Mash the flesh of the avocado until it is smooth. Mix with enough sour cream to bring it to a spreading consistency. Add the chopped parsley, and season with salt and pepper. Serve with toast or crispbread.

To prepare: 3 minutes

French Celeriac

Serves 4

This simple but tasty vegetable starter is based on a classic French recipe: personally I love it and can never eat enough of it!

1 large celeriac root
¼ pint/150 ml mayonnaise
curry paste

Peel the celeriac and cut it into thin slices. Cut these slices into long thin strips. Mix enough curry paste with the mayonnaise to give it quite a hot flavour, and mix in the celeriac strips. Chill.

To prepare: 4 minutes

Quick Cheese Straws

Makes 25-30

Irresistibly light and crunchy, these invariably vanish like dew before the morning sun.

5 oz/150 g plain flour
½ teaspoon (½ × 5 ml spoons) salt
4 oz/100 g Cheddar
¼ cup cooking oil
1½ tablespoons (1½ × 15 ml spoons) water

Pre-heat oven to gas mark 4/350°F/180°C

Sift the flour with the salt and stir in the grated cheese. Add the cooking oil and water and mix with your hands to a soft dough. Press into a 10 inch square baking dish and bake for 35 minutes. Cool a little, cut into squares, and leave until completely cold before removing from the tin.

To prepare: 3 minutes
Cooking time: 35 minutes

Sesame Sticks

Serve these either on their own as a cocktail nibble, or they are delicious with any of the avocado recipes.

4 slices of bread
butter
sesame seeds

Pre-heat oven to gas mark 6/400°F/200°C

Cut the crusts off the bread and flatten with a rolling pin. Butter the slices lavishly. Sprinkle thickly with sesame seeds and cut into sticks. Bake for 15-20 minutes until crisp. Cool in the tin.

To prepare: 4 minutes
Cooking time: 15-20 minutes

Special Consommé
Summer Soup
Pretty Gazpacho
Pimento Soup
Courgette Soup
Sugar Pea Soup
Spinach and Pea Soup
Leek Soup
Pumpkin Soup
Four Avocado Soups
Bread Fingers

Special Consommé

Serves 4

A very light way to start a meal, and with a touch of luxury. And the only action required is that of the tin-opener!

2 tins (15 oz/425 g) jellied consommé
4 tablespoons (4 × 15 ml spoons) double cream
1 small jar lumpfish roe
half a lemon

Serve the consommé, chilled and jellied, with a topping of thick cream and a few teaspoons of lumpfish roe. Decorate the edge of the dishes with twists of lemon.

To prepare: 1 minute
Chill for 2 hours

Summer Soup

Serves 6

Deliciously refreshing as a starter on balmy summer days, this soup has a mouthwatering contrast of textures.

2 tins (15 oz/425 g) jellied consommé
half a cucumber, diced
1 green pepper, shredded
2 tomatoes, skinned and chopped
half a ripe avocado, chopped

Melt the consommé over a gentle heat and add the vegetables. Chill until very cold and set. Serve sprinkled with fresh chives.

To prepare: 8 minutes
Chill for 2 hours

Pretty Gazpacho

The idea here is for each person to have a bowl of the tomato purée, and then you make up your own soup with the goodies on the platter: a friendly dish.

4 oz/100 g tinned tomatoes per person
garlic, salt and pepper

Liquidise the tomatoes with the juice in the tin and season to taste with crushed garlic, salt and pepper.

Serve with a platter of:
hard-boiled eggs
croûtons
pieces of crisped bacon
black olives
diced cucumber
sliced onion

To prepare: 10 minutes
Chill for 2 hours

Pimento Soup

Serves 4

This is unbeatable as a summer soup. It tastes as if you had spent hours of loving care adjusting flavours: but no, a minute's work, and this treat is yours.

1 large tin (14 oz/400 g) pimentoes
twice the volume of tomato juice
chopped chervil

Liquidise the pimentoes with the tomato juice and chill. Serve sprinkled with chopped chervil.

To prepare: 1 minute
Chill for 1 hour

Courgette Soup

Serves 4

Very light and summery, this is equally good hot or cold, and has a gentle flavour well matched to its beautiful pale greenness.

6 spring onions
1 lb courgettes
3 oz/75 g butter
½ pint/275 ml chicken stock
cream

Slice the spring onions and the courgettes and soften them in the melted butter for a few minutes until they begin to look transparent. Add the stock and simmer for 10 minutes. Liquidise, season to taste and finish with the cream.

To prepare: 12 minutes

Sugar Pea Soup

Serves 6

This is also delicious hot or cold: the soup retains, surprisingly, the nuttiness of the mange-tout peas, and is an excellent way of using frozen ones.

1 small onion
1½ oz/40 g butter
12 oz/350 g mange-tout peas
½ pint/275 ml stock
cream

Chop the onion finely and soften in the melted butter over a low heat. Toss the sugar peas in the butter for several minutes and then add the stock. Simmer for 10-12 minutes. Liquidise, strain through a sieve, and season to taste. Finish with cream.

To prepare: 15 minutes

Spinach and Pea Soup

Serves 4-6

This soup is sublime. There is no accounting for why, really, but it is one of the best in the world, wonderful either hot or cold.

2 oz/50 g butter
8 oz/225 g frozen peas
8 oz/225 g cooked spinach
1 pint/570 ml stock

Melt the butter and heat the frozen peas through in it until they are slightly softened. Add the spinach and mix well. Add the stock and liquidise.

To prepare: 5 minutes

Leek Soup

Serves 4

My very best leftovers-recipe. I actually cook more leeks than I need for one meal so that I can make this soup for the next day.

1 lb/450 g cooked leeks
1 pint/570 ml home-made stock
salt and pepper

Liquidise and heat through. Delicious.

To prepare: 2 minutes

Pumpkin Soup

This is another matter altogether. Adapted from a recipe of one of the great restaurants in France, this is a meal in itself and unless your appetite is gargantuan you can't possibly eat anything with it or after it. It is extremely rich and very greedy but it definitely makes it worthwhile falling into temptation from time to time.

1 good-sized pumpkin
4 large slices of bread, cut into dice
6 oz/175 g Gruyère cheese
1 pint/570 ml double cream
salt and pepper

Pre-heat oven to gas mark 3/325°F/170°C

Hollow out the seeds inside the pumpkin, reserving the top for a lid. Fill the cavity with alternate layers of the diced bread and the Gruyère cut into small cubes. Season the cream with salt and lots of black pepper, and pour it over the top inside the pumpkin. Put the lid back on and put in the oven for 2 hours. Serve up, using the pumpkin as a sort of soup bowl, scooping out the flesh and the now-gooey insides.

What a party dish this is, especially on Fireworks Night: you can leave it to cook itself whilst you enjoy the fun outdoors, and come in out of the cold for a truly memorable meal.

To prepare: 10 minutes
Cooking time: 2 hours

AVOCADO SOUPS

The versatility of the avocado is well-illustrated in these four soups: some are better hot than cold, and each one is entirely distinctive. They are quite rich and filling, so don't serve them in huge bowls if you want to enjoy your next course: a little goes a long way!

Plain Avocado Soup

Serves 4

1 large ripe avocado
1 tin (15 oz/425 g) consommé
1 small carton single cream
lemon juice
salt and pepper
pimento to garnish

Mash the flesh of the avocado and mix it with the consommé. Liquidise. Add the cream and lemon juice to taste, and season with salt and pepper. Chill. Serve garnished with strips of finely sliced pimento.

To prepare: 3 minutes
Chill for 2 hours

Avocado and Cucumber Soup

Serves 4

Definitely a summer soup, this one should be served chilled. Its taste is light and elusive and is highlighted by a garnish of chopped fresh chives.

1 cucumber
1 large ripe avocado
1 pint/570 ml stock
salt and pepper
chopped fresh chives

Peel and dice the cucumber and liquidise it with the mashed flesh of the avocado and the stock. Season to taste and serve chilled, sprinkled with the chopped chives.

To prepare: 3 minutes
Chill for 1 hour

Avocado and Watercress Soup

Serves 4

A lovely summer soup, either hot or cold: the spicyness of the cress is ideally wedded to the bland avocado.

1 bunch watercress
1½ oz/40 g butter
1 large ripe avocado
¾ pint/425 ml stock
cream

Chop the watercress very finely and simmer it in the melted butter for 5 minutes. Add the mashed avocado flesh and mix well. Thin out with the stock, liquidise, and finish with cream.

To prepare: 8 minutes

Avocado and Herb Soup

Serves 4

This is an original way of using garden herbs during the summer months when they are at their best. It is a favourite of mine and I like to use a mixture of lovage, chervil, dill, tarragon and chives.

1 bunch fresh herbs
1½ oz/40 g butter
1 large ripe avocado
½ pint/275 ml stock

Chop the herbs very finely and simmer for 5 minutes in the melted butter. Mash the avocado flesh and liquidise with the stock. Add the herbs, season to taste, and chill.

To prepare: 6 minutes
Chill for 1 hour

Bread Fingers

Serves 4

Simple as these are to prepare, they turn out to be little delicacies that go well with all the soups in this section.

Pre-heat oven to gas mark 3/325°F/170°C

Cut the crusts off slices of bread and cut into long thin fingers. Spread with garlic butter (see page 151). Place on a baking sheet and cook for 25 minutes until golden and crisp.

To prepare: a few minutes
Cooking time: 25 minutes

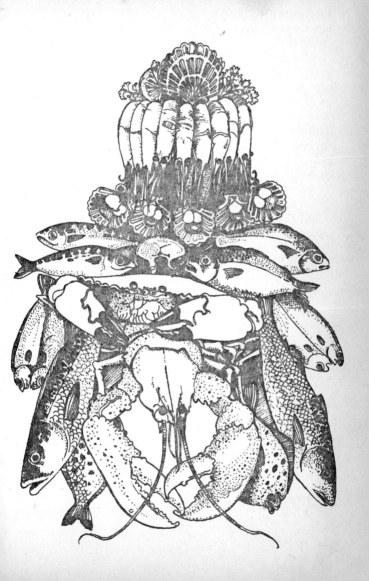

Crab Pâté and what to do with it
Avocado Crabs
Hot Avocado with Prawns
Avocado and Kipper Rolls
Kipper Puffs
Lemon Kippers
Smoked Mackerel and Prawn Pâté
Smoked Mackerel Pâté
Smoked Mackerel Salad
Pickled Mackerel
Marinated Plaice
Ritzy Sole
Tuna and Celery Salad
Tuna with Green Mayonnaise

For extra special occasions
Mussel Kebabs with Slivered Celeriac
Scallops with Vinegar and Slivered Turnip
Hubert's Snails

Crab Pâté and what to do with it

Serves 4

This is a light, tasty pâté easily made and very versatile too: you can serve it with toast, or with sticks of celery, or you can use it in the following avocado recipes.

1 good-sized crab, cooked
salt and pepper
4 oz/100 g unsalted butter
1 tablespoon (15 ml spoon) Worcester sauce
2 tablespoons (2 × 15 ml spoons) cream

Clean the flesh out of the crab and season it with salt and pepper. Mash it with the softened butter until smooth and creamy, and then mix in the Worcester sauce and cream. Chill. It freezes very well.

To prepare: 10 minutes

Avocado Crabs

The union of avocado and crab is legendary: here are two ways of bringing the avocado to your delicious crab pâté.

Way 1
Just fill the cavities of ripe, halved avocados with the pâté and serve on a lettuce leaf.

To prepare: 2 minutes

Way 2
Half a ripe avocado per person
salt and pepper
3 tablespoons (3 × 15 ml spoons) crab pâté per person
2 slivers of tomato per person
chopped fresh parsley
a twist of lemon

Mash the flesh of the avocado and line the bottom of a ramekin dish with it. Season with salt and pepper and cover with the pâté. Decorate with slivers of tomato, chopped parsley and a twist of lemon.

To prepare: 2 minutes

Hot Avocado with Prawns

Serves 4

Cold avocado with prawns is a well-known combination: but try using layers of both for a hot starter – it is a conversation-stopper.

2 small ripe avocados
salt and pepper
garlic butter (see page 151)
8 oz/225 g peeled prawns
lemon juice
breadcrumbs
butter

Pre-heat oven to gas mark 6/400°F/200°C

Peel the avocados and dice the flesh neatly. Put in the bottom of a ramekin dish and season liberally with salt and pepper. Pour a little garlic butter over the top. Make the next layer with the peeled prawns and season with pepper and lemon juice. Sprinkle with breadcrumbs and dot with butter. Put in a hot oven for 10 minutes and then finish quickly under a hot grill.

To prepare: 12 minutes
Cooking time: 10 minutes

Avocado and Kipper Rolls

Serves 4

A highly original starter, and one which you can adapt using smoked salmon.

1 ripe avocado
salt
lemon juice
Tabasco
olive oil
2 good kippers

Mash the flesh of the avocado to a purée, and season with salt, lemon juice and Tabasco. Thin out with a little olive oil. Cut the kippers in half and skin them. Cut them in half again, lengthwise, and put a spoonful of the avocado mixture on to the underside of each one. Roll them up, secure with a cocktail stick and serve with thinly sliced brown bread and butter on a bed of crisp lettuce and watercress.

To prepare: 10 minutes

Kipper Puffs
Serves 4

These are extraordinarily good: the kipper has acquired a pedestrian reputation but this dish elevates it to gastronomic status.

8 oz/225 g frozen puff pastry, defrosted
4 kipper fillets
lemon juice
cayenne pepper
butter
beaten egg

Pre-heat oven to gas mark 8/450°F/230°C

Roll the pastry out very thinly and cut into 4 inch (10 cm) squares. Place half a kipper fillet cut into small cubes on to each square and sprinkle with lemon juice and cayenne pepper. Put a knob of butter on top and fold over to make a pastry envelope. Seal the joins with water and press down with the tip of a fork. Brush the pastry with beaten egg and cook for 15 minutes or until golden. Allow to cool a little before serving. Allow two per person.

You can use smoked eel for this recipe, too; and smoked salmon 'pieces' – the inexpensive offcuts that you can buy at most fishmongers and some supermarkets – can boost this recipe right up-market!

To prepare: 8 minutes
Cooking time: 15 minutes

Lemon Kippers

Serves 4

This is an established favourite with many good cooks. It is a winner every time.

8 kipper fillets
1 large onion
pepper
2 lemons
¼ pint/150 ml olive oil

Slice the onion very thinly and place it over the kipper fillets in the bottom of a dish. Season well with black pepper. Squeeze the lemons and mix the juice with the olive oil. Pour over the fish fillets and marinate for 24 hours or even longer. Serve with thinly sliced brown bread and butter.

To prepare: 4 minutes
Marinate for 24 hours

Smoked Mackerel and Prawn Pâté

Serves 4

This is exquisite. The crunchy prawns make a delicious contrast with the light, moist paste. You can rely on it being different!

8 oz/225 g smoked mackerel
4 oz/100 g softened butter
1 tablespoon (15 ml spoon) olive oil
2 tablespoons (2 × 15 ml spoons) white wine
4 oz/100 g peeled prawns
4 tablespoons (4 × 15 ml spoons) double cream
cayenne pepper

Skin and fillet the smoked mackerel. Mash the butter with the oil and wine and beat the fish into this mixture until it is a fine paste. Mix in the prawns, add the cream and season to taste with cayenne pepper.

To prepare: 5 minutes

Smoked Mackerel Pâté

Serves 8

A standby that is always popular. You can make it whenever you are in the mood, and store it under a layer of clarified butter; or it freezes very well.

1 lb/450 g smoked mackerel
8 oz/225 g softened butter
a little cream
lemon juice
pepper

Skin the mackerel and lift out the backbone. Mix with the softened butter until the mixture is smooth and well-blended, removing any stray bones. Beat in a little cream. Season generously with lemon juice and freshly-ground black pepper. Serve chilled, with toast.

You can make a kipper pâté in exactly the same way.

To prepare: 4 minutes

Smoked Mackerel Salad

Serves 4

This recipe comes from the United States. It looks – and is – simple, and in simplicity is its success. It is a really delicious salad-starter.

1 lb/450 g smoked mackerel
1 bunch of watercress
2 sticks of chicory
4 oz/100 g almonds, browned under the grill
walnut or peanut oil
lemon juice
garlic

Skin the fish and cut it into bite-sized chunks. Mix with the watercress, sliced chicory and chopped nuts. Dress with walnut oil, lemon juice and a touch of garlic. Serve with warm wholemeal bread and butter.

To prepare: 5 minutes

Pickled Mackerel

Marinated fish is a great speciality of the Japanese, and personally I love the two following recipes. The fish retain a tempting texture and all their flavour, and are exquisitely transformed by the 'cooking' in the vinegar and lemon.

2 lb/1 kg fresh mackerel, filleted

For the marinade
1 large tablespoon (15 ml spoon) sea-salt
1 large tablespoon (15 ml spoon) sugar
1 teaspoon (5 ml spoon) ground pepper
½ pint/275 ml wine vinegar
juice of 1 lemon
1 bay leaf and 10 crushed allspice berries
thyme and other fresh herbs, finely chopped
1 clove garlic, chopped

Cut the mackerel fillets into 3 inch (7.5 cm) lengths. Mix all the marinade ingredients together. Lay the pieces of fish in the bottom of a dish and cover with the marinade and leave for at least 2 hours. Serve with fresh granary bread.

To prepare: 5 minutes
Marinate for 2 hours

Marinated Plaice

The fragile flavour of flat white fish is beautifully preserved in this marinade, and of course loses no moisture in the marinating process. It is astonishing how quickly it is 'cooked' by the wine and vinegar.

1 fillet of plaice per person

For the marinade
White wine to cover the fish
salt and pepper
chillis to taste
chopped shallots
chopped fresh herbs
a dash of wine vinegar

Mix the marinade ingredients together and place the fish, cut into thin slices, in it. Leave for a minimum of 15 minutes – but you can leave them for longer if it suits you, the fish will not spoil. Serve with crudités and brown bread.

You can also use this marinade to 'cook' very thin slices of fillet steak: the marinade transforms the meat, softens and flavours it. I love it like that, but then I'm a devotee of Steak Tartare as well! (see page 107).

To prepare: 2 minutes
Marinate for 15 minutes

Ritzy Sole

Serves 4

Wonderful, original, extraordinary. The longer you leave the cream mixture on the top the better it tastes. It softens and permeates the fish – food for the gods!

1 large lemon sole, filleted into 4
1 pint/570 ml water
6 tablespoons (6 × 15 ml spoons) wine vinegar
2 bay leaves
10 peppercorns
¼ pint/150 ml double cream
2 tablespoons (2 × 15 ml spoons) grated horseradish

Heat the water with the vinegar, bay leaves and peppercorns and simmer for 5 minutes. Turn the heat off and place the fillets, skin side up, in the hot liquid. Cover and leave to stand for 5 minutes. Drain and cool. Skin the fillets and put on to a pretty plate.

Whip the cream and mix in the horseradish. Spread a layer over each of the fillets and sprinkle with chopped parsley. Chill for as long as possible.

To prepare: 12 minutes
Chill for 2 hours minimum

Tuna and Celery Salad

Serves 4

Contrasting textures and tastes here, with the tang of fresh herbs: a lovely summer starter.

1 large tin tuna
4 tablespoons (4 × 15 ml spoons) wine vinegar
4 tablespoons (4 × 15 ml spoons) French mustard
8 sticks of celery
fresh herbs

Cut the fish into very small pieces and season with half the vinegar and mustard mixed together. Chop the celery very finely and toss in the other half. Mix the two together and add the finely chopped herbs – I like to use tarragon, chervil, parsley and chives. Stir well and serve in little salad bowls.

To prepare: 5 minutes

Tuna with Green Mayonnaise

Serves 4

Straight from the larder shelf but it works wonders on the taste-buds, the gentleness of the tuna being a lovely base for the strong flavours of the herbs.

1 large tin tuna
a bunch of fresh herbs
4 tablespoons (4 × 15 ml spoons) mayonnaise
salt and pepper
lemon juice
2 hard-boiled eggs
2 tomatoes
1 small chopped onion

Drain the tuna and mash it. Chop the herbs finely and mix into the mayonnaise, and season with salt, pepper and lemon juice. Place the fish in the centre of a platter and cover with the herb mayonnaise. Surround with the sliced eggs and tomatoes and chopped onion.

To prepare: 5 minutes

FOR EXTRA-SPECIAL OCCASIONS

Mussel Kebabs with Slivered Celeriac   Serves 1

You can buy packets of frozen mussels to save the time of preparing them yourself – and they're always on hand as they defrost very rapidly. They are far superior to the jars of mussels in brine and make excellent kebabs.

10 mussels
2 shallots
2 oz/50 g mushrooms
6 slices of celeriac
olive oil

Pre-heat grill to moderate heat

Quarter the mushrooms, and thinly slice the shallots. Peel and finely slice the celeriac and cut to the same size as the mussels. Alternate the vegetables and mussels along a skewer, brush with olive oil and turn under the grill for about 5 minutes. Serve with wedges of lemon, and spiced rice.

You can make all sorts of variations on this recipe: try adding scallops to the skewer, or smoked oysters (which are sensational), or both. Some supermarkets sell frozen oysters: that would do for a really extra-special occasion!

To prepare: 3 minutes
Cooking time: 5 minutes

Scallops with Vinegar and Slivered Turnip   Serves 1

The credit for this dish goes to Bistro Hubert in Paris where I once had a most memorable meal whilst on holiday. This is my version of what they served me as a main course.

3 scallops
1 oz/25 g butter
salt and pepper
lemon juice
1 tablespoon (15 ml spoon) wine vinegar

1 baby turnip
a dash of cream

Slice the scallops fairly thinly and sauté very lightly in the butter. Season with salt and pepper, and lemon juice. Add the vinegar to the pan and cook gently for 3 minutes. Meanwhile slice the baby turnip finely and cut these slices into thin strips. Add to the pan and cook for another 2 minutes. Add the cream, heat through and serve immediately. The dish needs no accompaniment.

To prepare: 3 minutes
Cooking time: 8-10 minutes

Hubert's Snails

Serves 2

From the same restaurant – this was the first course so you can tell what a good meal I had! Garlic butter is the classic sauce for snails, and an excellent one – but this is sheer ambrosia.

2 oz/50 g butter
1 large clove garlic
½ oz/12 g ground almonds
½ oz/12 g slivered almonds
a dash of cream

Pre-heat oven to gas mark 3/325°F/170°C

Melt the butter, crush the garlic and add it to the butter with the ground almonds. Stir over a low heat for 2 minutes. Add the slivered almonds, then the cream, heat through and pour a little of the sauce over each snail in its shell and heat through in the oven for 10 minutes. Enough for 12 snails.

Of course it is not easy to come by snails – edible ones at any rate – in this country, so what I do whenever I am in France on holiday is to nip into a supermarket and buy half a dozen tins of snails so that I have a supply on the larder shelf to keep me going until the next holiday!

To prepare: 3 minutes
Cooking time: 10 minutes

VEGETABLE STARTERS IN AN INSTANT

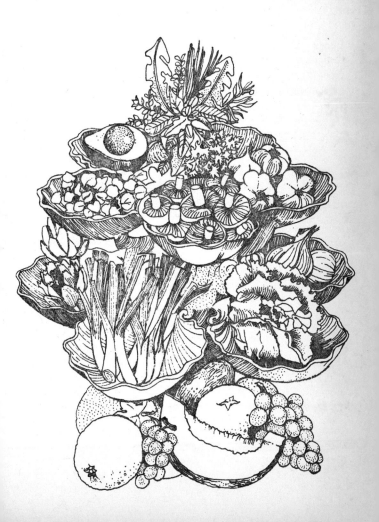

Grapefruit Cocktail
Salade des Vignerons
Lettuce Hearts with Bacon
Lettuce Hearts with Nuts
Mushrooms in a Case
Stuffed Mushrooms
Mushrooms with Pesto
Melizanes Salata
Leeks with Soft-boiled Eggs
Artichokes with Garlic Butter
Avocado with Garlic Butter
Avocado with Watercress

Grapefruit Cocktail

Serves 1

Summery, refreshing and appetising: a delightfully light way to start a meal.

½ grapefruit
¼ melon, diced
10 grapes, skinned and with the pips removed
vinaigrette dressing (see page 151)

Remove the fruit from the grapefruit shell and chop it. Mix with the melon and grapes and return to the shell. Dress with a very garlicky vinaigrette and serve chilled.

To prepare: 5 minutes
Chill for at least 1 hour

Salade des Vignerons

Serves 4

This recipe, as its name reveals, is French, and is quite a country classic. The sharpness of the dandelion leaves is delicious with the fat of the bacon, so cast timidity to the winds and try it!

1 endive lettuce and a few dandelion leaves
olive oil
salt and pepper
6 oz/175 g streaky bacon
2 tablespoons (2 × 15 ml spoons) vinegar

Prepare the lettuce and the dandelion leaves and dress them with the oil, salt and pepper. Cut the bacon into tiny dice and fry in its own fat until it is brown and crisp all over. Pour the vinegar into the pan and sizzle until well-reduced. Pour over the salad, toss well and serve immediately.

To prepare: 10 minutes

Lettuce Hearts with Bacon

Serves 1

Lettuces are utterly changed by cooking and I often think it's a shame that we don't think of them as a cooked vegetable, but always as a salad. The flavour is enhanced and the texture softened and they are beautiful just plain with butter, or with bacon and nuts as in this recipe.

1 lettuce heart
salt and pepper
1 oz/25 g streaky bacon
a few roasted peanuts
grated Parmesan cheese

Pre-heat oven to gas mark 6/400°F/200°C

Season the lettuce heart and put it in an ovenproof dish with a little water. Cover with foil and bake for 25 minutes. Meanwhile crisp the bacon and crumble it when it has cooled. Sprinkle over the lettuce heart with the chopped nuts and cheese and serve immediately.

To prepare: 5 minutes
Cooking time: 25 minutes

Lettuce Hearts with Nuts

Serves 1

Another example of the excellence of cooked lettuce, but cold this time. Cook the lettuce heart as above, and serve it cold sprinkled with finely chopped walnuts and a herb vinaigrette made with walnut or peanut oil.

To prepare: 3 minutes
Cooking time: 25 minutes

Mushrooms in a Case

Serves 4

Garlic and mushrooms bring out the best in each other, and slipped into a toasted hollowed-out roll they make a mouth-watering starter.

4 large mushrooms
salt and pepper
2 small round rolls
garlic butter (see page 151)

Pre-heat oven to gas mark 4/350°F/180°C

Season the mushrooms with salt and pepper, cover with foil and bake for 30 minutes. Halve and hollow out the rolls so that you have a round shell, and pop them in the oven for 10 minutes to crisp up. Put the cooked mushrooms into the bread shells, pour over the melted garlic butter and serve at once.

To prepare: 6 minutes
Cooking time: 30 minutes

Stuffed Mushrooms

Serves 4

Mushroom-lovers beware of your waistline . . .

8 oz/225 g large flat mushrooms
8 oz/225 g streaky bacon
garlic and basil to taste
salt and pepper
grated Parmesan cheese
breadcrumbs
butter

Pre-heat oven to gas mark 6/400°F/200°C

Remove the stalks from the mushrooms and place the caps in a well-buttered dish.

For the stuffing: Cook the bacon in its own fat until very crisp, and crumble it when cooled. Add to the very finely chopped mushroom stalks cooked in butter with garlic and chopped basil. Add a little grated Parmesan and fill the caps with this mixture. Sprinkle with breadcrumbs, dot with butter and bake for 10-15 minutes.

To prepare: 5 minutes
Cooking time: 10-15 minutes

Mushrooms with Pesto

Serves 4

A wonderful use for pesto. The basil and the garlic do everything for the mushrooms.

12 oz/350 g mushrooms
salt and pepper
pesto (see page 83)

Pre-heat oven to gas mark 5/375°F/190°C

Wipe the mushrooms and put into an ovenproof dish. Season with salt and pepper, cover with foil and bake for 15 minutes. Remove from the dish, and toss quickly in a little pesto before serving warm in ramekin dishes.

To prepare: a few minutes
Cooking time: 15 minutes

Melizanes Salata

Serves 6

This brings back memories of Greece, of lazy lunches in the shade after long mornings swimming in the Mediterranean. And then walking up into the hills . . .

2 aubergines
1 tablespoon (15 ml spoon) breadcrumbs
1 clove garlic
1 small chopped onion
1 tablespoon (15 ml spoon) chopped thyme
salt and pepper
½ cup olive oil
juice of half a lemon

Pre-heat oven to gas mark 4/350°F/180°C

Bake the aubergines for 40 minutes. Cool and remove the skin. Soak the breadcrumbs in water and squeeze them dry. Put the aubergines, breadcrumbs, garlic, onion and thyme in the blender and season to taste. Add the oil to the purée gradually, as if for mayonnaise. Then add the lemon juice and thin out if necessary with a little water. Serve cold with melba toast or pitta bread, and a bottle of retsina.

To prepare: 5 minutes
Pre-cook for 40 minutes

Leeks with Soft-boiled Eggs

Serves 4

An elegant dish: soft-boiled eggs and the distinctive flavour of leeks are well-balanced and please the palate.

8 leeks
4 eggs
parsley to garnish

Cook the leeks until tender. Meanwhile, boil the eggs for 3 minutes and then plunge into cold water. Peel them carefully and place each egg in the centre of a small warmed plate. Make a circle around it with the leeks, garnish with parsley and serve with fresh bread.

To prepare: 15 minutes

Artichokes with Garlic Butter

Serves 1

When the artichoke season is with us I cannot eat too many of them, either with plain melted butter, or cold with vinaigrette, or even with hollandaise. But try them hot with garlic butter!

1 artichoke
1 oz/25 g garlic butter (see page 151)

Boil the artichoke in salted water for 40 minutes or until well done right through. Serve with the garlic butter and dip each leaf into it. When you get to the heart you are in for a treat!

To prepare: 3 minutes
Cooking time: 40 minutes

Avocado with Garlic Butter

A must. If you've never had avocado hot, this is the recipe to start with. You will be converted!

Pre-heat oven to gas mark 5/375°F/190°C

Halve a ripe avocado and take out the stone. Make lengthwise cuts into the flesh and fill the hole in the middle with garlic butter (see page 151). Bake for 10-15 minutes. Allow one half avocado per person.

To prepare: 1 minute
Cooking time: 10-15 minutes

Avocado with Watercress

Serves 2

A dish to stun your guests: the cress-flavour livens up the avocado in this sophisticated partnership.

1 ripe avocado
1 bunch watercress
1½ oz/40 g butter

Pre-heat oven to gas mark 6/400°F/200°C

Cut the avocado in half and bake it for 15 minutes. Meanwhile chop the watercress finely and simmer it gently in the melted butter. Fill the cavities of the avocado with this mixture and serve immediately, with fresh bread.

To prepare: 3 minutes
Cooking time: 15 minutes

Chinese Prawn Omelette
Baked Eggs with Ham
Poached Eggs in Tomatoes
Fried Eggs with a Difference
Scrambled Eggs with Smoked Eel
Pipérade
Tuna and Anchovy Omelette
Jellied Eggs with Salami and Avocado

Chinese Prawn Omelette

Serves 1

I love Chinese food and enjoy my westernised version of cooking it:
it is light, quick and always tasty.

2 Chinese leaves
half a small onion
a little parsley
soy sauce
salt, pepper and garlic to taste
3 oz/75 g peeled prawns
butter
2 eggs
cream or top of the milk

Chop the leaves, onion and parsley finely and marinate in soy sauce
for an hour with the crushed garlic, salt and pepper. Sauté the
prawns for a minute or two in butter, then stir in this mixture and
warm through. Beat the eggs and add a little cream or milk, season
with salt and pepper and make the omelette in the usual way, filling
it with the prawn mixture. Serve with a tomato salad and fresh
bread.

To prepare and marinate: 1 hour
Cooking time: 6 minutes

Baked Eggs with Ham

Serves 1

Served with fresh bread, a green salad and a glass of red wine, this is
the quickest and easiest of lunches.

2 eggs
salt and pepper
butter
2 oz/50 g ham

Pre-heat oven to gas mark 8/450°F/230°C

Butter some small ramekin dishes and break an egg into each one. Season with salt and pepper and cook for 7 minutes. Meanwhile heat some more butter and let it sizzle until it turns brown. Cut the ham into thin strips and heat it through in the butter. Garnish the eggs with the ham strips and serve at once.

To prepare: 2 minutes
Cooking time: 7 minutes

Poached Eggs in Tomatoes   Serves 1

I think that poached eggs are a great dish: slipped into a hollowed-out Mediterranean tomato they are sublime.

half a large Mediterranean tomato
butter
1 egg
salt and pepper
fresh herbs

Hollow out the tomato and turn it gently in melted butter to soften it, and save the juices in the pan. Meanwhile poach the egg, slip it into the tomato shell and pour the juices over the top. Sprinkle with salt and pepper and finely chopped herbs of your choice. Serve with toast and a mixed salad.

To prepare: 5 minutes

Fried Eggs with a Difference

Serves 1

The sophisticated touch of vinegar and parsley redeems this dish from the realms of the crude and makes it perfectly excusable!

2 eggs
olive oil
salt and pepper
1 tablespoon (15 ml spoon) vinegar
fresh chopped parsley

Heat the oil in a frying pan and fry the eggs so that they crisp up around the edge. As they are cooking, season them with salt and pepper and add the vinegar to the pan. Let it sizzle merrily, and then serve the eggs on hot plates sprinkled with chopped parsley. Eat with fresh bread and a salad of your choice (see Salads At Full Speed, page 127).

To prepare: 3 minutes

Scrambled Eggs with Smoked Eel

Serves 1

Scrambled eggs come a close second to poached eggs in my esteem. And I will find any excuse to eat smoked eel: the two together are pure luxury.

2 eggs
cream or top of the milk
salt and pepper
butter
2 oz/50 g smoked eel

Beat the eggs with the cream or milk and season with salt and pepper. Heat the butter in a heavy saucepan until it turns brown, then turn the heat down a little and cook the eggs, stirring all the time. As they begin to set, stir in the chopped smoked eel and finish cooking, being careful not to let the eggs get too dry. Serve your creamy mixture on toast, with a side-salad.

To prepare: 4 minutes

Pipérade

Serves 1

I remember my mother often making this French regional dish for a
quick lunch, and I have always loved its tang.

1 oz/25 g ham
quarter of a green pepper
2 tomatoes
butter and oil
2 eggs
salt and pepper

Cut the ham into strips, chop the pepper, and skin and chop the
tomatoes. Melt the butter with the oil and cook the ham and pepper
in it for 5 minutes. Add the tomatoes, season well, and cook for a few
more minutes. Beat the egg-whites, mix with the yolks and scramble
with the mixture in the pan. Cook until just set and serve at once on
warm plates. Delicious on toast with a salad and cold white wine.

To prepare: 12 minutes

Tuna and Anchovy Omelette

Serves 2

An unusual combination for an omelette, you might think, but
unusually delicious.

1 small tin tuna fish
6 anchovy fillets
2 shallots
half a small glass white wine
1 oz/25 g butter
4 eggs

Drain the fish and chop it finely. Chop the anchovies. Slice the
shallots and cook them in the white wine until it is well-reduced.
Add the butter to the pan and when it has melted stir in the tuna and
the anchovies. Make the omelette in your usual way, fill with the fish
mixture and serve immediately.

To prepare: 5 minutes

Jellied Eggs with Salami and Avocado

Serves 4

This is my version of some beautifully-prepared 'oeufs en gelée' that I bought from a French charcuterie on holiday once: but I can never get them to look quite as professional as the experts do!

1 tin (15 oz/425 g) consommé
4 eggs
4 very thin slices of salami
half an avocado
4 tablespoons (4 × 15 ml spoons) mayonnaise

Soft-boil the eggs for 4 minutes, plunge them into cold water and peel them very carefully when they are cold. Put a slice of salami on the bottom of one ramekin dish per person, place an egg on top and surround with slivers of avocado. Heat the consommé gently, then fill each ramekin up and leave to cool and set. Decorate with piped mayonnaise, and serve chilled with salad and bread fingers (see page 40).

To prepare: 10 minutes
Chill for 2 hours

FONDUES ARE FUN

Cheese Fondue with Cider
Cheddar Fondue with Beer
Cauliflower Fondue
Anchovy and Garlic Fondue
Aioli with Raw Vegetables

Fondues are a friendly way of eating: there is a special communion about eating from the same pot, and I like the informality too. The classic steak fondue makes a memorable meal but these days it also makes a memorable hole in the bank balance. These three recipes are kinder to the housekeeping, and very simple to prepare – although it's the vegetables that take the time!

Vegetables to Serve with Fondues and Dips

cucumber
carrots
peppers
French beans
celery
spring onions
lettuce

mushrooms
cauliflower
tomatoes
courgettes
chicory
beetroot

Cheese Fondue with Cider

Serves 4

2-3 teaspoons (5 ml spoons) cornflour
1 teaspoon (5 ml spoon) dry mustard
pepper
½ pint/275 ml dry cider

Mix the dry ingredients to a smooth cream with a little of the cider.
Set aside.

1 oz/25 g butter
1 lb/450 g Cheddar, grated

Melt the butter in a fondue pot, add the cheese and the remaining
cider and heat gently, stirring all the time until it is smooth. Add the
flour mixture, then turn up the heat a little and stir until it thickens.
Bubble gently and serve with raw vegetables (see above) and little
squares of fresh bread to dip into the pot.

To prepare: 6 minutes

Cheddar Fondue with Beer

Serves 4

1 cut clove garlic
½ pint/275 ml beer
12 oz/350 g Cheddar, grated
1 tablespoon (15 ml spoon) flour
1 teaspoon (5 ml spoon) Worcester sauce

Rub the fondue pot with the garlic. Pour in the beer and bring it to
the boil. Mix the cheese with the flour and add gradually to the beer,
stirring until it becomes smooth. Add the Worcester sauce, bring to
the boil and serve in the fondue pot with raw chopped vegetables and
little squares of fresh bread to dip in.

To prepare: 6 minutes

Cauliflower Fondue

Serves 4

To either of the fondues above add 12 oz/350 g blanched cauliflower florets and serve simply with fingers of toast.

Anchovy and Garlic Fondue

Serves 4

This calls for candlelight: it is exquisite and has never failed to be a success in my experience.

2 oz/50 g butter
8 anchovy fillets
1 large clove of garlic
¾ pint/425 ml double cream

Melt the butter over a low heat and add the anchovy fillets, rinsed and chopped so finely that they are almost a pulp. Stir in the finely chopped garlic and simmer for a little while. Heat the cream in the fondue pot, add the anchovy mixture and stir well. Serve with bread sticks and raw vegetables.

To prepare: 8 minutes

Aioli with Raw Vegetables

Serves 4

My favourite summer standby: and there is no doubt that – if you have the time – it is best made with home-made mayonnaise.

2 large cloves of garlic
¾ pint/425 ml mayonnaise

Crush the garlic and add to the mayonnaise. Leave in a cool place whilst you prepare the raw vegetables to dip into it (see above). Serve with French bread and a lusty red wine.

To prepare: 10 minutes

Kidney Kebabs
Liver and Ham Kebabs
Sausage and Bacon Kebabs
Ham and Cheese Kebabs
Fish and Bacon Kebabs
Shellfish Kebabs

Kebabs undoubtedly taste best when they are cooked over a summer barbecue, sprinkled with aromatic herbs and eaten 'al fresco'. But they are also memorable and quick standbys in less clement weather, and the shellfish kebab is a classic for all seasons.

Kidney Kebabs

Serves 1

2 rashers of bacon
4 mushrooms
2 tomatoes
half an onion
salt and pepper
olive oil
dried herbs

Slice all the ingredients and skewer alternately on to kebab sticks.
Season with salt and pepper, brush with olive oil and grill, turning
occasionally, for about 10 minutes. Sprinkle dried aromatic herbs
over towards the end of the cooking time.

To prepare: 5 minutes
Cooking time: 10 minutes

Liver and Ham Kebabs

Serves 1

3 oz/75 g lamb's liver
2 oz/50 g ham
2 oz/50 g mushrooms
olive oil
dried herbs
fresh sage leaves
melted butter
fresh parsley

Slice the liver and the ham and quarter the mushrooms. Marinate in
oil and herbs for 1 hour. Stick on to kebab skewers alternately, and
put sage leaves between some of the slices. Brush with melted butter
and grill gently for 10-12 minutes, turning occasionally, until the
liver is cooked through but not dry. Serve garnished with finely
chopped parsley, and tarragon butter (see page 151).

Marinate for 1 hour
Cooking time: 12 minutes

Sausage and Bacon Kebabs

Serves 1

2 spicy sausages
2 rashers of bacon
quarter of a green pepper
half an onion
2 bay leaves
salt and pepper
olive oil

Slice all the ingredients except the bay leaves. Skewer alternately on to kebab sticks and season with salt and pepper. Brush with olive oil and grill for 15-20 minutes, turning from time to time.

To prepare: 5 minutes
Cooking time: 15-20 minutes

Ham and Cheese Kebabs

Serves 1

This one is obviously not a kebab for the barbecue! From the fire back to the frying pan, you might say.

2 oz/50 g sliced ham
3 oz/75 g Gruyère cheese
beaten egg
flour
oil
fresh parsley

Cut the ham into squares and wrap up cubes of Gruyère inside them to make little parcels. Stick on to kebab skewers, dip in beaten egg and flour, and fry for about 6 minutes, turning in the hot oil. Serve sprinkled with parsley and a side salad of tomato and onion rings.

To prepare: 5 minutes
Cooking time: 6 minutes

Fish and Bacon Kebabs

Serves 1

6 oz/175 g white fish
4 rashers of bacon
2 tomatoes
4 mushrooms
salt and pepper
olive oil

Stretch the rashers of bacon with the back of a knife and cut them in half across. Wrap chunks of the fish in the bacon, and put on to skewers with alternating quarters of tomato and mushroom. Season, brush with olive oil and grill for 10-12 minutes under a fairly hot grill.

To prepare: 5 minutes
Cooking time: 12 minutes

Shellfish Kebabs

For when you are feeling extravagant, generous, or just downright greedy!

Alternate on skewers chunks of scallops, large prawns, monkfish, and even such delicacies as langoustines or lobster tails. Put between them slices of bacon, onion, and quartered mushrooms. Brush with masses of melted butter and sprinkle with finely chopped fresh herbs. Grill gently, turning until the fish is cooked through. Serve with spiced rice and a green salad.

To prepare: 5 minutes
Cooking time: 10 minutes

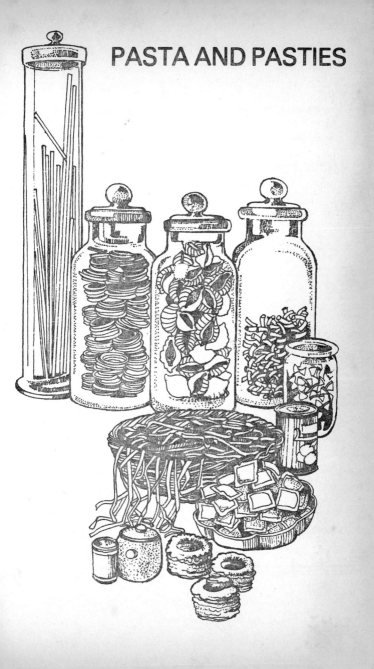

PASTA AND PASTIES

Pasta Pesto
Pasta Ricardo
Pasta with Avocado Sauce
Leek and Smoked Oyster Vol-au-Vent
Mushroom Vol-au-Vents
Chicken and Tarragon Vol-au-Vents
Cheese Pasties
Mushroom Pasties
Shellfish Pasties with Beansprouts

PASTA

You should allow 4 oz/100 g pasta (uncooked) per person and cook
your chosen variety until it is 'al dente'.

Pasta Pesto

Serves 2

Pesto is my favourite sauce. I love basil, and grow masses of it every
year. At the end of the season of fresh salads I use whatever leaves I
have left to make pesto to see me through the winter months.

For the pesto:
1 large bunch of fresh basil
2 large cloves of garlic
4 oz/100 g walnuts
¼ pint/150 ml olive oil
2 oz/50 g grated Parmesan cheese

Liquidise the basil, garlic, nuts and oil. Stir in the Parmesan. You
can store the pesto in screw-top jars in the fridge almost indefinitely.

Cook your chosen pasta, noodles or spaghetti 'al dente' and toss
with a generous quantity of pesto. Serve immediately on hot plates.

To prepare: 3 minutes
Cooking time for the pasta: 10-15 minutes

Pasta Ricardo

Serves 2

Ricardo's recipe is beguilingly simple and turns the most restrained
eater into a monster of greed.

1 tin anchovies
¼ pint/150 ml olive oil
1 large clove garlic
8 oz/225 g pasta shapes

Chop the anchovy fillets into ½ inch (1 cm) lengths. Heat the olive oil with the crushed garlic over a gentle heat, add to the anchovies and heat through, being careful not to overcook or else the anchovies will dissolve. Pour over your freshly-cooked pasta, toss and serve immediately.

To prepare: 3 minutes
Cooking time: 10-15 minutes

Pasta with Avocado Sauce   Serves 2

This sauce is lovely either on plain tagliatelle, or on stuffed pasta such as ravioli or rigatoni.

half a ripe avocado
salt and pepper
garlic
Tabasco
½ pint/275 ml stock
2 tablespoons (2 × 15 ml spoons) thick cream

Mash the avocado and season to taste with salt and pepper, crushed garlic and Tabasco. Gradually thin it out with hot stock, beating all the time to keep it smooth. When it is the consistency of thick cream, add the cream, adjust the seasoning and heat through. Serve on freshly-cooked pasta as a main course.

To prepare: 5 minutes
Cooking time: 10-15 minutes

VOL-AU-VENTS

You can buy such good frozen vol-au-vent cases to keep in the freezer that you can make these delicacies in a matter of minutes – and there is no end to the variation of fillings you can try. Here are four of my favourites.

Leek and Smoked Oyster Vol-au-Vent

Serves 4

Definitely a party-piece.

1 8-10 inch/20-25.5 cm vol-au-vent case (pre-cooked)
1 lb/450 g leeks
1 can smoked oysters
⅓ pint (200 ml) béchamel sauce
cream

Pre-heat oven to gas mark 5/375°F/190°C

Cook the leeks until tender and shred them. Mix them into the béchamel sauce and add a little cream. Mix in the chopped smoked oysters with a little of the juice from the can. Season the mixture to taste, fill the case, put the lid on top and bake for 25 minutes.

To prepare: 15 minutes
Cooking time: 25 minutes

Mushroom Vol-au-Vents

Serves 4

A delicious lunch or supper dish, served with a fresh green salad.

8 individual vol-au-vent cases (pre-cooked)
1½ lb/700 g mushrooms
8 oz/225 g butter
garlic
salt and pepper

Pre-heat oven to gas mark 5/375°/190°C

Chop the mushrooms finely and cook in the butter until they are soft. Season with salt and pepper and crushed garlic to taste. Liquidise. Fill the vol-au-vent cases with the mixture and heat through in a hot oven for 10-15 minutes.

To prepare: 5 minutes
Cooking time: 10-15 minutes

Chicken and Tarragon Vol-au-Vents

Serves 4

This is an excellent way of using up leftover chicken.

8 vol-au-vent cases (pre-cooked)
1 lb/450 g cold cooked chicken
a little cream
¼ pint/150 ml béchamel sauce
a small bunch of fresh tarragon

Pre-heat oven to gas mark 5/375°F/190°C

Chop the chicken and mix with a little béchamel. Heat a little cream and cook the chopped tarragon in it for a few minutes. Add to the chicken and use as a filling for individual vol-au-vent cases. Heat through for 10-15 minutes.

To prepare: 10 minutes
Cooking time: 10-15 minutes

PASTIES

Frozen puff pastry to the rescue again! It is far better than any puff pastry I have ever managed to make myself, and saves hours of work.

Cheese Pasties

Serves 4

These melt in the mouth and are dangerous for slimmers.

8 oz/225 g frozen puff pastry
12 oz/350 g cheese

Pre-heat oven to gas mark 7/425°F/220°C

Roll the pastry out thinly and cut into 4 inch (10 cm) squares. Put 1½ oz/40 g of cubed cheese on to each square (you can use Cheddar, Gruyère, Bel Paese or Roquefort), wet the edges and fold into a triangle. Press the edges together with a fork, brush with beaten egg and bake in the oven for 10-15 minutes until puffed and golden.

To prepare: 5 minutes
Cooking time: 10-15 minutes

Mushroom Pasties

Make exactly as for the cheese pasties above, using a filling of 2 oz/ 50 g chopped mushrooms per pasty, cooked in butter with chopped spring onion and parsley.

Shellfish Pasties with Beansprouts   Serves 4

8 oz/225 g frozen puff pastry
4 oz/100 g chopped prawns
4 oz/100 g crabmeat
2 oz/50 g beansprouts
2 oz/50 g mussels
1 scallop
butter
2 tablespoons (2 × 15 ml spoons) béchamel sauce
beaten egg

Pre-heat oven to gas mark 7/425°F/220°C

Toss the prawns, crabmeat, beansprouts, mussels and sliced scallop in melted butter, and add the béchamel to bind the mixture. Roll out the puff pastry thinly and cut into four 4 inch (10 cm) squares and place a quarter of the mixture on to each one. Fold over into triangles, seal the edges with water and press together with a fork. Brush with beaten egg and cook for 10 minutes.

To prepare: 10 minutes
Cooking time: 10 minutes

NIMBLE FISH DISHES

Prawns in Garlic and Ginger
Boozy Prawns
Avocado with Prawns and Mushrooms
Smokies with Cheese
Peppery Smoked Mackerel
Cod Cutlets with Nutty Butter
Creamy Trout
Trout in a Shirt
Red Mullet with Basil Butter
Grilled Plaice with Green Butter
Mackerel with Bacon
Whiting with Quick Garlic Sauce

Prawns in Garlic and Ginger

Serves 2

Garlic and ginger are a classic combination in Chinese cookery, and although this quick and easy recipe has no pretensions to being *haute cuisine*, it is nevertheless remarkably good.

6 oz/175 g soft Chinese noodles (cook while you prepare the prawns)
1 large clove of garlic
1 oz/25 g green ginger
2 shallots
8 oz/225 g shelled prawns
salt and pepper
pinch of sugar
oil
4 tablespoons (4 × 15 ml spoons) cream

Sauté the finely chopped garlic, ginger and shallots in oil. Add the prawns and toss, cooking for 2 minutes. Season with salt and pepper and a pinch of sugar, and stir in the cream. Heat through and serve with the noodles.

To prepare: 6 minutes
To cook noodles: 5 minutes

Boozy Prawns

Serves 2

I love this dish, it is the perfect answer to a special meal 'à deux', served with rice and a green salad. You can also use this mixture as a filling for hot avocados, as a starter.

6 oz/175 g rice
2 oz/50 g butter
8 oz/225 g shelled prawns
1 large measure of whisky
½ pint/275 ml double cream
salt and pepper

Cook the rice for 10-15 minutes. Meanwhile, melt the butter in a frying pan and when it is quite hot toss the prawns in it until they are heated through. Pour on the whisky and flambé. When the flames have died down stir in the cream, heat through and allow to bubble for a little while. Season to taste and serve on a bed of plain rice.

To prepare: 6 minutes
To cook rice: 10-15 minutes

Avocado with Prawns and Mushrooms   Serves 2

This recipe is, like the one above, ideal for intimate dinners. Its special ingredients and unusual combinations of taste and texture are enhanced by candlelight.

1 small avocado
salt and pepper
4 oz/100 g mushrooms
1 oz/25 g butter
8 oz/225 g prawns
black pepper
garlic
breadcrumbs

Pre-heat oven to gas mark 5/375°F/190°C

Mash the avocado and season it well with salt and pepper. Spread it over the bottom of a small baking dish. Cover with a layer of the mushrooms, thickly sliced and cooked quickly in the butter so that they are still crisp. Season well and cover with the prawns. Sprinkle with freshly ground black pepper and crushed garlic and top with breadcrumbs. Dot with butter and bake for 20 minutes.

To prepare: 10 minutes
Cooking time: 20 minutes

Smokies with Cheese

Serves 4

Smokies, always delicious, are made even more so by this light mixture of eggs and cheese which is rather like Welsh rarebit.

4 smokies
¼ pint/150 ml top of the milk
1 oz/25 g butter
lemon juice
black pepper
2 oz/50 g grated cheese
2 beaten eggs

Pre-heat oven to gas mark 4/350°F/180°C

Put the fish into an ovenproof dish and cover with the milk. Dot with butter, season with lemon juice and black pepper and cover with foil. Bake the fish for 15-20 minutes, and then remove them from the dish and split them open. Beat the eggs and mix in the cheese, put the fish into a heatproof dish, and cover with this mixture. Cook under the grill until the cheese has browned and the eggs are set.

Cooking time: 25 minutes

Peppery Smoked Mackerel

Serves 4

This unusual treatment of smoked mackerel gives it glamour and style.

4 fillets of smoked mackerel
1 oz/25 g mixed black peppercorns, white peppercorns, juniper berries and allspice berries
2 bay leaves
2 oz/50 g butter

Pre-heat oven to gas mark 4/350°F/180°C

Place the mackerel fillets skin-side down in a heatproof dish. Pound and crush the spices in a mortar and sprinkle over the fish. Dot with butter and tuck the bay leaves in between the fillets. Cover with foil and heat through for 12 minutes.

To prepare: 3 minutes
Cooking time: 10 minutes

Cod Cutlets with Nutty Butter   Serves 4

I have made this dish for the poshest of dinner parties and it has always been praised to the skies; but there is nothing to it.

4 cod cutlets
juice of 2 lemons
salt and pepper

Sprinkle each cod cutlet with lemon juice all over and season with salt and pepper. Grill under a moderate grill until just done through but not too dry and flaky. Meanwhile, prepare the Beurre Noisette to be served with the fish.

Beurre Noisette
Heat 4 oz/100 g of butter in a heavy pan until it sizzles madly and goes brown and frothy. Pour immediately over the cod cutlets.

Cooking time: 5-7 minutes

Creamy Trout   Serves 4

This delicate treatment for trout has a finesse that suits its delicate flavour and makes it melt in the mouth.

4 oz/100 g butter
4 trout, cleaned
8 oz/225 g button mushrooms
½ pint/275 ml double cream
pepper
1 lemon

Melt half the butter and pour it into a heatproof dish. Turn the trout in the butter and lay them in the dish under the grill. Turn when they start to go golden – after about 8 minutes, and then place the mushrooms, lightly cooked in butter and still whole, over the top. Pour on the cream, season with pepper and grill for another 8 minutes or until the trout are cooked through. Serve with wedges of lemon.

Cooking time: 15 minutes

Trout in a Shirt

Serves 4

Although this recipe is simplicity itself, in my opinion it is one of the very best ways of cooking trout.

4 trout, cleaned
6 oz/175 g butter
juice of 2 lemons
chopped fresh parsley
salt and pepper

Pre-heat oven to gas mark 5/375°F/190°C

Mash the butter with most of the juice of the lemons and the chopped parsley, salt and pepper. Put a quarter of this mixture inside each of the trout, season with salt and pepper and the remaining lemon juice on the outside, and wrap up each fish in foil. Cook for 15-20 minutes.

To prepare: 4 minutes
Cooking time: 20 minutes

Red Mullet with Basil Butter

Serves 4

I had this dish in a Paris restaurant years ago, and to this day I remember every detail of it. The fish had been briefly finished on charcoal, and that aroma, combined with the fragrance of basil, was utterly memorable.

4 medium red mullet, cleaned
4 large sprigs of fresh basil
salt and pepper
juice of 2 lemons

Pre-heat oven to gas mark 4/350°F/180°C

Put a sprig of basil inside each fish and season its skin with salt, pepper and lemon juice. Wrap each one up in foil and cook for 15-20 minutes. Meanwhile make the basil butter.

Basil Butter
1 large bunch fresh basil
4 oz/100 g butter
salt and pepper

Chop the basil finely. Melt the butter over a gentle heat and season with salt and pepper. Add the chopped basil, stir until well-mixed, and pour over the cooked fish. Put under a hot grill for a minute and then serve immediately.

To prepare: 2 minutes
Cooking time: 15-20 minutes

Grilled Plaice with Green Butter

Serves 4

This herb sauce, with its added bite of anchovy and capers, livens up flat white fish immensely.

4 large plaice
juice of 2 lemons
salt and pepper

Season each fish with salt, pepper and lemon juice, and grill for several minutes on each side until the fish is cooked. Meanwhile prepare the green butter.

Green Butter
a few sprigs each of fresh tarragon, chervil, parsley and fennel
1 shallot
4 oz/100 g butter
3 anchovy fillets
1 tablespoon (15 ml spoon) capers
2 gherkins, very finely chopped
salt and pepper

Finely chop the herbs and slice the shallot thinly. Melt the butter and simmer these in it for a few minutes. Add the finely chopped anchovy fillets, the capers and gherkins and season with salt and pepper. It is ready to serve with the fish.

Cooking time: 8 minutes

Mackerel with Bacon   Serves 4

Spring onions and bacon complement the full flavour of mackerel, making this a wonderful main course.

2 fresh mackerel, cleaned
8 rashers of bacon
10 spring onions
juice of 2 lemons

Pre-heat oven to gas mark 6/400°F/200°C

Cut the heads and tails off the mackerel and cut them in half lengthwise. Remove the backbone. Grease a flameproof dish and sprinkle with the chopped spring onions. Season the fish and place on the onions. Stretch the rashers of bacon with the back of a knife and cover each piece of fish with two rashers. Cook for 15 minutes. Remove the fish from the pan and keep warm, and crisp the bacon under the grill for a minute or two. Add the lemon juice to the juices in the pan and boil over a hot flame until well reduced and then pour over the fish and serve, garnished with the bacon.

To prepare: 5 minutes
Cooking time: 20 minutes

Whiting with Quick Garlic Sauce

Serves 4

I've always thought whiting to be underestimated: certainly with this garlic sauce it will surprise its critics.

4 good-sized whiting, cleaned
salt and pepper
juice of 2 lemons

Season the fish well all over with salt, pepper and lemon juice. Grill on both sides until cooked through, about 10 minutes. Meanwhile prepare the Garlic Sauce.

Garlic Sauce
1 oz/25 g flaked almonds
2 large cloves of garlic
½ pint/275 ml stock
3 tablespoons (3 × 15 ml spoons) breadcrumbs
little cream or top of the milk, to finish

Liquidise all the ingredients and then stir over a gentle heat for 10 minutes. Finish with a little cream or top of the milk and serve.

To prepare and cook: 15 minutes

Devilled Kidneys
Kidneys with Green Peppercorns
Kidneys in their Jackets
Mustardy Liver
Liver with Avocado Slivers
Tongue with Mushrooms
Sweet and Sour Turkey Fillets
Turkey Breasts in Pastry
Run Rabbit Run
Pork Fillet with Mushrooms
Veal Escalopes with Sorrel
Steak with Avocado Crust
Avocado Carpaccio
Steak Tartare

Kidneys respond well to the 'quick and memorable' style of cooking, and to my mind are far better fresh than frozen. Liver likewise is incomparably better fresh, and the recipes included here are really quite gastronomic for humble offal! Turkey is a great personal favourite of mine, and can make dishes fit for a king, as can tender pork fillet and escalopes of veal. Neither of these two need long cooking, otherwise they become dry and boring, so cook them lightly and they will retain their mouthwatering texture. And for when you want to pull out all the stops, both financial and gastronomic, here are three steak recipes which will make your meals memorable meals indeed!

Devilled Kidneys

Serves 4

1 lb/450 g lamb's kidneys

For the butter:
1 small bunch fresh parsley
1 shallot
1 small piece root ginger
2 tablespoons (2 × 15 ml spoons) mustard
salt and pepper
2 oz/50 g softened butter

Chop the parsley and shallots, shred the ginger, and mix with the mustard, salt and pepper. Mash into the softened butter.

Cut the kidneys into slices and spread them with the butter. Leave for an hour to marinate. Grill, turning once, until they are cooked through but still pinkish.

To prepare: 5 minutes
Marinate for 1 hour
Cooking time: 8 minutes

Kidneys with Green Peppercorns

Serves 4

An excellent dish for a dinner party.

1 lb/450 g lamb's kidneys
salt and pepper
2 oz/50 g green peppercorns
4 oz/100 g butter
½ pint/275 ml double cream

Slice the kidneys and season with salt and pepper. Crush the green peppercorns in a mortar. Toss the kidneys in melted butter until they are lightly cooked, then add the green peppercorns and the cream. Stirring gently, heat through for a few minutes, and serve.

You can add lightly sautéed mushrooms to the sauce if you like, to add another texture.

To prepare: 3 minutes
Cooking time: 5-8 minutes

Kidneys in Their Jackets

Serves 2

6 lamb's kidneys, still coated in their layer of suet fat.

Pre-heat oven to gas mark 8/450°F/230°C

Trim the fat around the kidneys to a thin layer and bake for 30-40 minutes, basting from time to time. Serve very hot.

Cooking time: 30-40 minutes

Mustardy Liver

Serves 2

8 oz/225 g lamb's liver
salt and pepper
flour
2 oz/50 g butter
2-3 tablespoons (15 ml spoons) mustard
¼ pint/150 ml single cream

Cut the liver into long thin slices and season well. Toss in flour and sauté quickly in hot butter just to sear the outside but leaving the inside pink. Remove the liver to a hot dish. Add the mustard to the juices in the pan, stir well and add the cream. Heat through, season to taste and pour over the liver. Serve at once.

To prepare: 2 minutes
Cooking time: 5 minutes

Liver with Avocado Slivers

Serves 2

8 oz/225 g lamb's or, for a treat, calf's liver
1 avocado
salt and pepper
2 oz/50 g butter
a little lemon juice

Warm the avocado in a low oven whilst you prepare and cook the liver.

Cut the liver into thin slices and season well with salt and pepper. Fry it very lightly in a little hot butter and then sprinkle with lemon juice. Serve covered with slices of the warm avocado. Delicious with fresh bread and a chicory salad.

To prepare: 1 minute
Cooking time: 3-5 minutes

Tongue with Mushrooms

Serves 2

I regard tongue as a great speciality: its texture and flavour are in a category all of their own. This is more of a memorable snack than a meal, but worth including none the less.

2 slices of bread
2 slices of tongue
2 large mushrooms
salt and pepper
butter

Pre-heat oven to gas mark 6/400°F/200°C

Butter the bread and place the slices of tongue on them to cover them. Place the whole mushroom caps without their stalks on the top and season with salt and pepper. Dot with butter and bake for 20 minutes.

To prepare: 3 minutes
Cooking time: 3-5 minutes

Sweet and Sour Turkey Fillets

Serves 4

8 oz/225 g mushrooms
4 oz/100 g butter
4 fillets of turkey breast
salt and pepper
flour
8 tablespoons (8 × 15 ml spoons) vinegar
8 tablespoons (8 × 15 ml spoons) brown sugar
12 oz/375 g noodles, cooked for 5-7 minutes while you prepare the
    turkey

Sauté the sliced mushrooms in very hot butter, very quickly so that
they are still crisp. Slice the fillets of turkey breast into long strips,
season well and roll in flour. Cook very rapidly in hot, browned
butter, turning until the meat is seared. Add the vinegar and allow to
bubble. Add the brown sugar and stir until blended. Mix in the
mushrooms and dish up. Serve with the soft noodles.

Cooking time: 10 minutes

Turkey Breasts in Pastry

Serves 4

4 good-sized slices of turkey breast
salt and pepper
8 oz/225 g puff pastry
1 egg yolk

Pre-heat oven to gas mark 6/400°F/200°C

Season the turkey slices well with salt and pepper. Roll out the puff
pastry thinly and wrap up each slice in a parcel, sealing the edges
with water and pressing them down with a fork. Glaze with the
beaten egg yolk. Cook for 20-25 minutes until the pastry is golden
and cooked through.

To prepare: 5 minutes
Cooking time: 20-25 minutes

Run Rabbit Run

Serves 4

You can buy excellent frozen Chinese rabbit nowadays which I find to be as good as – if not better than – chicken. It is delicious barbecued, and also super with this herb sauce

1 lb/450 g boneless rabbit
2 oz/50 g butter
a bunch of fresh lovage or tarragon
a little flour
½ pint/275 ml top of the milk
salt and pepper

Cut the rabbit into little slivers and cook gently in half of the butter for 10 minutes, turning occasionally. Meanwhile chop the lovage or tarragon very finely and wilt it in the rest of the butter. Sprinkle on a little flour and stir until smooth, then gradually add the top of the milk, stirring until it thickens. Simmer for a few minutes and season to taste. Add the rabbit with its juices from the pan and mix thoroughly. You have a delectable dinner.

Cooking time: 15 minutes

Pork Fillet with Mushrooms

Serves 4

8 oz/225 g mushrooms
4 oz/100 g butter
1 lb/ 450 g pork fillet
salt and pepper
½ pint/275 ml double cream

Slice the mushrooms and sauté them lightly in butter. Set aside. Slice the pork into pieces about ½ inch (1 cm) thick, season and cook quickly in the butter, allowing just a minute or two so that the meat does not dry out. Add the mushrooms to the pan, pour on the cream and heat through. Serve at once on a bed of boiled rice.

To prepare: 4 minutes
Cooking time: 3 minutes

Veal Escalopes with Sorrel

Serves 4

4 veal escalopes
salt and pepper
4 oz/100 g butter
a large bunch of sorrel

Season the meat and cook in the hot butter until well done through but not dry. Meanwhile cook the sorrel with a little water and a knob of butter, stirring well until it breaks down to a purée. Add the pan juices from the veal, stir, and cover the escalopes with the purée. Serve immediately.

Cooking time: 8 minutes

Steak with Avocado Crust

Serves 2

This is unusual and delectable. In moments of abandoned extravagance you can do the same thing with lobster: it is delicious.

1 ripe avocado
salt and pepper
garlic
Tabasco
8 oz/225 g fillet of beef, cut into two steaks

Mash the avocado and season to taste with salt, pepper, garlic and Tabasco. Grill the steak as required, then spread the avocado paste over the steak so that it is about ¼ inch thick. Return to the grill and cook until the avocado has browned and heated through, which will take several minutes.

To prepare: 3 minutes
Cooking time: 5 minutes

Avocado Carpaccio

Serves 4

1 ripe avocado
8 oz/225 g fillet steak
1 bunch watercress

For the vinaigrette
oil
garlic
vinegar
salt and pepper

Slice a ripe avocado and marinate it in the vinaigrette for a minimum of two hours.

Freeze the fillet steak until it is hard. Slice it, frozen, in paper-thin slices like Parma ham. Leave to thaw.

Arrange the slices of avocado and steak on a bed of watercress, and serve with fresh bread and gherkins.

To prepare: 5 minutes
Marinate the avocado for 2 hours
Freeze the steak for 4 hours

Steak Tartare

Serves 2

8 oz/225 g raw fillet steak, minced
1 raw egg yolk
a dash of Worcester sauce
salt and pepper
a pinch of English mustard
1 small onion, minced
paprika, to taste
1 tablespoon (15 ml spoon) tomato purée
1 tablespoon (15 ml spoon) chopped fresh parsley
1 tablespoon (15 ml spoon) capers
grated rind of half a lemon
1 tablespoon (15 ml spoon) olive oil

Mix all the ingredients together and serve decorated with radishes and slices of tomato.

An exotic restaurant in Paris adds brandy, chopped anchovies and garlic to their Steak Tartare. Nobody has ever taken me there and I haven't tried it out myself, but it sounds as if it could be a memorable experience.

To prepare: 6 minutes

DOUBLE QUICK CHICKS

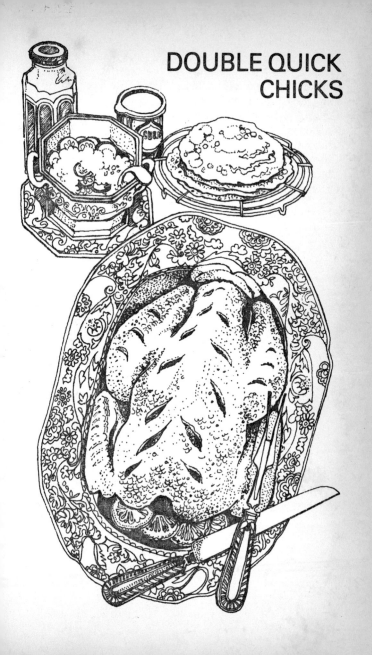

Chicken with Baby Sweetcorn
Chicken with Water Chestnuts
Chicken with Oatmeal and Water Chestnut Stuffing
Pan-fried Chicken with Lettuce
Grilled Chicken with Garlic Butter
Tandoori Chicken
Chicken with Green Peppercorns
Chicken Cucumber Mayonnaise
Chicken and Avocado Mayonnaise
Chicken Mayonnaise with Anchovy

Chicken with Baby Sweetcorn

Serves 2

You can buy cans of baby sweetcorn from all Chinese supermarkets and some delicatessens, so here's a hint of the Orient straight off the larder shelf.

2 chicken breasts
salt and pepper
3 oz/75 g butter
2 tablespoons (2 × 15 ml spoons) wine vinegar
1 small tin baby sweetcorn
4 spring onions

Slice the chicken and season with salt and pepper. Melt the butter in a heavy pan and heat it until it turns brown and begins to sizzle and froth. Add the vinegar and let it rage and storm a little. Then turn down the heat and cook the chicken breasts lightly until done through but not dry. Remove and keep warm. Heat the baby sweetcorn in the juices in the pan, pour over the chicken and garnish with finely chopped spring onions.

To prepare: 4 minutes
Cooking time: 6 minutes

Chicken with Water Chestnuts

Serves 2

Water chestnuts are another speciality that you can store on the larder shelf. Their crunchiness in contrast to the chicken on its bed of soft noodles, makes this dish irresistible.

12 oz/350 g chicken breasts
salt and pepper
3 oz/75 g Beurre Noisette (see page 94)
6 oz/175 g water chestnuts
6 oz/175 g soft noodles, cooked for 5-7 minutes whilst the chicken is prepared and cooked.

Slice the chicken and season with salt and pepper. Cook in the Beurre Noisette fairly briefly so that it remains moist and pinkish, about 4 minutes, and towards the end of the cooking time add the finely sliced water chestnuts. When they are warmed through, serve on the bed of soft noodles.

To prepare: 4 minutes
Cooking time: 8 minutes

Chicken with Oatmeal and Water Chestnut Stuffing

Serves 4

This stuffing is so easy to prepare, and so delicious, that it is an established favourite of mine. It is lovely eaten cold, with leftovers, the next day.

4 oz/100 g butter
4 oz/100 g medium oatmeal
1 onion, chopped
lots of fresh herbs, chopped
salt and pepper
8 water chestnuts

Melt the butter and stir in the oatmeal. Add the chopped onion, herbs and seasonings. Slice the water chestnuts and cut them into thin strips and stir in. Stuff a 4 lb/2 kg chicken and roast as usual.

To prepare: 5 minutes

Pan-fried Chicken with Lettuce

Serves 4

Cooked lettuce is a treat – it has a surprisingly individual flavour and adds colour and interest to this simple dish.

1 lb/450 g chicken breast meat
4 oz/100 g butter
salt and pepper
lemon juice
16 lettuce leaves

Slice the chicken meat and sauté in melted butter and then season with salt, pepper and lemon juice. Remove from the pan and keep warm. Shred the lettuce coarsely and cook in the pan juices until softened. Line the bottom of a warm dish with this mixture and lay the chicken slices on top. Serve with soy sauce.

Cooking time: 6 minutes

Grilled Chicken with Garlic Butter

Serves 4

This is astonishingly sophisticated for something which is fundamentally such a simple idea.

4 chicken drumsticks
salt and pepper
4 oz/100 g garlic butter (see page 151)

Season the drumsticks with salt and pepper and grill them all round until the skin is crisp and golden and the meat cooked. Pour the garlic butter over them and leave under a very low grill for 5 minutes. Lovely served with pasta and all the garlicky juices.

Cooking time: 15 minutes

Tandoori Chicken

Serves 4

4 whole chicken legs
2 tablespoons (2 × 15 ml spoons) curry paste
½ pint/275 ml natural yogurt

Pre-heat oven to gas mark 4/350°F/180°C

Cut neat gashes into the chicken with a sharp knife. Mix the curry paste into the yogurt and marinate the chicken pieces in it over-night. It tenderises the meat and the spices permeate it with their flavours. Place the chicken, still coated in the yogurt, in a baking tray and cook for 40 minutes. Serve with poppadoms and a mixed salad.

Marinate overnight
Cooking time: 40 minutes

Chicken with Green Peppercorns

Serves 4

The gentle spiciness of green peppercorns gives this dish great distinction and I often serve it as a main course for a party.

1 oz/25 g green peppercorns
4 oz/100 g butter
4 oz/100 g mushrooms
2 boneless chicken breasts
1 small carton of double cream

Crush the peppercorns and heat them in 1 oz/25 g of the butter, and in a separate pan sauté the sliced mushrooms in the rest of the butter – very quickly so that they are still crisp. Remove from the pan and sauté the seasoned slices of chicken until they are lightly cooked. Pour on the cream and stir well. Then add the green peppercorn and butter mixture, mix well, heat through and serve at once.

To prepare and cook: 12 minutes

Chicken Cucumber Mayonnaise

Serves 2

8 oz/225 g cooked chicken
1 cucumber
¼ pint/150 ml mayonnaise
cream
salt and pepper
vinegar

Shred the chicken. Peel the cucumber and cut it into little squares and cook these in boiling water to which you have added salt and a little vinegar. Boil for 3 minutes and then drain and cool. Mix the chicken and the cucumber with the mayonnaise and a little cream, and season to taste.

To prepare: 8 minutes

Chicken and Avocado Mayonnaise

Serves 2

1 large avocado
12oz/350 g cooked chicken
salt and pepper
crushed garlic
¼ pint/150 ml mayonnaise
chopped fresh marjoram

Mash the avocado and season it well with salt and pepper and garlic. Shred the chicken and mix with the mayonnaise. Cover the avocado with the chicken and sprinkle with the marjoram.

To prepare: 6 minutes

Chicken Mayonnaise with Anchovy

Serves 2

8 oz/225 g cooked chicken
1 can anchovy fillets
¼ pint/150 ml mayonnaise
chopped fresh parsley
salt and pepper

Shred the chicken. Chop the anchovy fillets very finely indeed and mix into the mayonnaise with the oil from the can. Add the chicken and mix well. Season to taste and serve sprinkled with chopped parsley.

To prepare: 6 minutes

THE VEGETABLE EXPRESS

Purées
Creamy Cabbage
Lettuce in Cream
Braised Lettuce Hearts
Chicory with Cream
Soy-braised Cabbage
Cauliflower with Nutty Butter
Grated Carrots Baked in Butter
Artichokes Fried with Garlic
Fried Cucumber
Courgettes Vincenzo
Instant Ratatouille
Baked Mushrooms
Mushroom Casserole

Purées

Purées are almost my favourite way of eating vegetables, and they are especially useful for using up leftovers. I liquidise the cooked vegetables with some of their cooking juices or stock, and add a little butter. If the vegetables are good then there is no need to season the purée – just eat it as it is. Here are some vegetables to try:

Carrots, leeks, cauliflower with watercress, root artichokes, celeriac, peppers, potato with sorrel, Brussels sprouts, turnips.

Creamy Cabbage   Serves 4-6

This is the best luxury way of cooking cabbage that I know, and wonderfully rich and satisfying it is. Serve it with plain grilled meat or fish, or on its own as a starter.

1 medium white cabbage
4 oz/100 g butter
black pepper
1 pint/570 ml double cream
croûtons

Parboil the uncut cabbage in salted water for 6 minutes, then let it cool and chop it finely. Melt the butter in the pan and add the shredded cabbage. Cook very slowly until tender. Season liberally with black pepper. Add the cream and heat through. Serve sprinkled with croûtons.

To prepare: 6 minutes
Cooking time: 6 minutes

Lettuce in Cream

Serves 4

My enthusiasm for cooked lettuce is unbounded, and these two recipes will surely convince the unconverted of its excellence.

2 lettuces
4 oz/100 g butter
salt
½ pint/275 ml double cream
croûtons

Shred the lettuce and melt the butter over a gentle heat. Put in the lettuce and stir gently. Then turn the heat right down, season with a little salt, and cover the pan. Simmer until the lettuce moisture has been absorbed, about 5 minutes. Add the cream, stir well, heat through and serve with croûtons.

Cooking time: 5 minutes

Braised Lettuce Hearts

Serves 4

8 lettuce hearts
4 oz/100 g butter
salt and pepper

Season the hearts with salt and pepper. Cook them in the butter over a gentle heat, turning, until they are softened but still crisp inside – just a few minutes. Serve at once.

Cooking time: 3-4 minutes

Chicory with Cream

Serves 4

In my view chicory is infinitely better cooked than raw. Much as I love it in salads, when cooked it acquires a delicate flavour which makes it the peer of asparagus.

8 sticks of chicory
8 oz/225 g butter
salt
sugar
juice of half a large lemon
½ pint/275 ml double cream

Pre-heat oven to gas mark 3/325°F/170°C

Heat the butter in a casserole dish and toss the whole sticks of chicory in it. Season with salt, sugar and lemon juice. Add the cream, cover the dish with foil and cook for 20-25 minutes in a slow oven.

To prepare: 3 minutes
Cooking time: 20-25 minutes

Soy-braised Cabbage

Serves 4

The touch of soy sauce and garlic in this recipe makes this cabbage dish a sensational companion to roast meats.

1 medium cabbage
4 tablespoons (4 × 15 ml spoons) cooking oil
a little water
soy sauce
1 chicken stock cube
2 oz/50 g butter
salt and pepper
garlic

Shred the cabbage and toss in the heated oil. Add a little water, soy sauce to taste, the stock cube and butter. Season with salt and pepper and garlic then cook, uncovered, for 10 minutes.

To prepare: 2 minutes
Cooking time: 10 minutes

Cauliflower with Nutty Butter

Serves 4-6

The simple ploy of pouring browned butter over lightly cooked cauliflower quite transforms it.

1 cauliflower
4 oz/100 g butter

Cook the cauliflower florets 'al dente'. Meanwhile heat the butter and cook it until it foams and turns nut-brown. Pour over the cooked florets and serve at once.

Cooking time: 5 minutes

Grated Carrots Baked in Butter

Serves 4

Try serving these scrumptious carrots with one of the kidney dishes on page 101.

1 lb/450 g raw carrots
salt and pepper
finely chopped fresh herbs
4 oz/100 g melted butter

Pre-heat oven to gas mark 4/350°F/180°C

Grate the carrots, season them well with salt and pepper and mix in some finely chopped fresh herbs. Toss in the melted butter until thoroughly coated and cook in an open dish for 15 minutes.

To prepare: 4 minutes
Cooking time: 15 minutes

Artichokes Fried in Garlic

Serves 4

Food for the gods, and especially delicious with red meats.

1 lb/450 g Jerusalem artichokes
3 oz/75 g butter
crushed garlic

Peel the Jerusalem artichokes and cook in boiling water until they are done through but still slightly crisp. Drain and slice them. Melt the butter over a medium heat and toss the artichoke slices in it until well coated. Add as much garlic as you like, stir well and allow to cook gently for another minute or two.

To prepare: 15 minutes

Fried Cucumber
Serves 4

One of the most delicious things in the world.

1 cucumber
3 oz/75 g butter
salt and pepper

Peel the cucumber and cut it into slices about ¾ inch/2 cm thick. Melt the butter in a pan and toss the slices briefly in it until the cucumber begins to soften but is still just crisp inside. Season to taste and serve. A feast.

To prepare: 3 minutes
Cooking time: 5 minutes

Courgettes Vincenzo
Serves 2-3

This recipe comes from a restaurant in sun-drenched Positano. It is a meal in itself and I often make it in the summer when there is a glut of courgettes. To ring the changes you can substitute aubergines for the courgettes.

1 lb/450 g courgettes
12 oz/350 g tomatoes
8 oz/225 g Mozzarella cheese
olive oil
salt and pepper
garlic

Pre-heat oven to gas mark 4/350°F/180°C

Cut the courgettes into slices about ½ inch (1 cm) thick and fry in olive oil until they are browned and softened. Make layers in a baking dish of the courgette slices, the skinned and sliced tomatoes and the sliced Mozzarella. Season each layer with salt and pepper and garlic, and finish with a layer of the cheese. Bake for 30 minutes.

To prepare: 10 minutes
Cooking time: 30 minutes

Instant Ratatouille
Serves 2

Accusations of 'Cheating!' have to be met here with a defence case of quick and easy, and quite delicious!

1 8 oz/225 g tin tomatoes
half a cucumber
2 small onions
garlic to taste
chopped fresh herbs
salt and pepper

Chop the tomatoes, peel and dice the cucumber and slice the onions. Add the garlic, herbs and seasonings and simmer together for 10 minutes.

To prepare: 5 minutes
Cooking time: 10 minutes

Baked Mushrooms
Serves 4

If you are going to cook mushrooms at all – after all they are so good raw! – this is undoubtedly one of the best ways of retaining maximum flavour.

Pre-heat oven to gas mark 4/350°F/180°C

Put 1 lb/450 g cleaned mushrooms into an ovenproof dish, sprinkle with salt and pepper and cover with foil. Bake for 20 minutes.

Cooking time: 20 minutes

Mushroom Casserole

Serves 2

If you can find wild mushrooms, this is an excellent way of cooking them. Otherwise little button mushrooms are very good.

8 oz/225 g small mushrooms
2 oz/50 g butter
¼ pint/150 ml double cream
juice of half a lemon

Pre-heat oven to gas mark 6/400°F/200°C

Sauté the whole mushrooms in butter for 1 minute. Drain off the juices, season and put into 2 little ramekin dishes. Mix the lemon juice with the cream, pour over the mushrooms, and bake for 12 minutes.

To prepare: 3 minutes
Cooking time: 12 minutes

Avocado Salads
Clever Ways with Cucumber
Cauliflower Salad
Italian Salad
Grilled Pepper and Mushroom Salad
Lemon Salad
Trinity Salad
Turnip Salad
Parisian Cabbage Salad
Carrot and Beansprout Salad
Courgettes with Fines Herbes
Roquefort and Walnut Salad
Spinach, Mushroom and Bacon Salad
French Bean Salad

Avocado Salads

Possibilities with avocados are boundless. In salads, they can be mixed with all kinds of vegetables, dressed with differingly seasoned vinaigrettes and mayonnaises, and served either as side dishes or as starters. Try them – sliced or diced – with leeks and walnuts in a garlicky vinaigrette; with artichokes, in a mustardy dressing. With broad beans, celery and herbs, or with baby turnips and finely chopped fresh parsley. Avocado with raw mushrooms in a garlicky vinaigrette on a bed of lettuce is irresistible, or try it with crispy lettuce and herbs in a garlic mayonnaise. With tomatoes and chives in vinaigrette, or with fennel root, lettuce and walnuts in mayonnaise: the variations expand. Try it with orange and chives and chopped almonds, or as a light salad with cucumber and herbs in vinaigrette. For a delicious and more substantial dish mix diced avocado with cooked pasta, dressed in masses of pesto (see page 83). Salads for all seasons!

Clever Ways with Cucumber

Cucumber is always light and refreshing, and as a side salad it goes with almost everything – cheese, eggs, fish, chicken and red meats.

Way 1
Grate a cucumber and sprinkle it with salt. Season with lemon juice or vinegar, a little oil and chopped chervil. Add crushed garlic to taste. Leave for 10 minutes before serving.

To prepare and marinate: 12 minutes

Way 2
Thinly slice two cucumbers and mix with a carton of sour cream. Season with salt, lemon juice, chopped onion and dill pickle, pepper and chopped fresh parsley. For a touch of the Orient add 1 tablespoon (15 ml spoon) sesame seeds.

To prepare: 5 minutes

Way 3

Peel and dice a cucumber. Mix with half a carton of yogurt, 1 small clove of garlic, crushed, and lots of chopped fresh dill. Season to taste and chill until ready to serve.

To prepare: 5 minutes

Way 4

Peel a cucumber and slice it very finely. Mix 1 tablespoon (15 ml spoon) Dijon mustard with some vinegar, salt and pepper, and 1 tablespoon (15 ml spoon) sugar. Marinate the slices for as long as you want and you have a sort of sweet and sour cucumber.

To prepare: 4 minutes

Cauliflower Salad   Serves 4

A stylish winter salad, this, and useful as a starter as well as being a tasty side-salad.

1 cauliflower
2 oz/55 ml walnut oil
juice of half a lemon
salt and pepper
2 oz/50 g walnuts
watercress to garnish

Parboil the florets of the cauliflower so that they are still crisp and nutty – a matter of a very few minutes. Make a vinaigrette with the walnut oil and lemon juice and seasonings, and dress the cauliflower with it. Sprinkle with the finely chopped walnuts and surround with sprigs of watercress.

To prepare: 6 minutes

Italian Salad

I ate this at an immaculate Italian restaurant in London years ago, and have never forgotten how good it was. It consisted of sliced fennel, green and red peppers, celery and young celery leaves, celeriac and crisp lettuce. Everything was cut into long thin strips and tossed in French dressing with a little chopped spring onion as garnish.

To prepare: 10 minutes

Grilled Pepper and Mushroom Salad   Serves 3-4

The strong aftertaste of peppers combined with the gentle delicacy of mushrooms goes beautifully with light chicken and fish dishes. It is also very good on its own, as an hors d'oeuvre.

2 green peppers
1 red pepper
8 oz/225 g mushrooms
vinaigrette (see page 151)
fresh parsley

Cut the peppers into quarters, take the seeds out and grill skin-side up for about 5 minutes, until the skin has blistered. Remove the skin and cut the flesh into long thin strips. Slice the mushrooms, mix with the peppers and dress with vinaigrette. Sprinkle with chopped parsley and serve.

To prepare: 10 minutes

Lemon Salad   Serves 4

This unusual salad is delicious with Grilled Chicken with Garlic Butter (see page 113).

4 lemons, unpeeled
2 oz/50 g roasted almonds
1 ripe avocado
vinaigrette (see page 151)
chopped herbs

Boil the lemons until they are soft in a lot of salty water, about 20 minutes. Drain and cool, and then slice them. Chop the almonds and mix with the lemons. Peel and slice the avocado and mix in. Dress with vinaigrette and sprinkle with the chopped herbs.

To prepare: 25 minutes

Trinity Salad
Serves 3-4

A classic salad that is a light meal in itself: an excellent lunch dish served with French bread and chilled white wine.

1 cos lettuce
12 spring onions
8 oz/225 g Cheddar, finely grated
lots of oil and vinegar to taste
salt and pepper
crushed garlic

Blend the grated cheese with oil, vinegar, seasoning and garlic to taste, as if for a mayonnaise. Mix with the shredded lettuce and chopped spring onions when you are ready to serve it.

To prepare: 8 minutes

Turnip Salad
Serves 2-3

I always thought I hated turnips until I experimented with this recipe: it is sublime and I am converted.

12 tiny young turnips
¼ pint/150 ml mayonnaise
curry paste
2 tablespoons (2 × 15 ml spoons) apricot jam

Cut the raw turnips into long thin strips. Mix the mayonnaise with curry paste to taste. Heat the apricot jam, sieve it and strain into the mayonnaise. Stir in well and dress the turnip with the mixture.

To prepare: 5 minutes

Parisian Cabbage Salad

Serves 3-4

The idea for this simple salad comes from a little restaurant in Paris where the chef prepared it so lovingly and prettily that I have never forgotten it.

half a white cabbage
6 spring onions
fresh parsley
1 small cucumber
garlic vinaigrette (see page 151)

Shred the cabbage very finely into long thin strips. Mix in the finely chopped spring onions, chopped parsley and peeled and grated cucumber. Leave to macerate for a while in the garlicky vinaigrette.

To prepare: 5 minutes

Carrot and Beansprout Salad

Serves 4

Simplicity itself, but a nutritious and adaptable side-salad.

8 oz/225 g carrots
8 oz/225 g beansprouts
1 bunch watercress
4 oz/100 g radishes
1 lettuce
garlic vinaigrette (see page 151)

Grate the carrots and mix with the chopped watercress and beansprouts. Slice the radishes and toss in. Dress with a very garlicky vinaigrette and serve on a bed of lettuce.

To prepare: 6 minutes

Courgettes with Fines Herbes

I never tire of courgettes and I prepare them in all kinds of ways; this is so simple to do when the herbs in the garden are at their height, and there is the usual summer glut of courgettes. I make it over and over again and always enjoy it.

Slice raw courgettes very finely, as paper thin as possible, and dress with a garlicky vinaigrette. Sprinkle with chopped fresh herbs of your choice and it is ready to serve.

To prepare: 4 minutes

Roquefort and Walnut Salad   Serves 2

This salad is not for timid taste-buds. I think that the best way to serve it is as a starter for hungry people on chilly evenings.

2 slices of bread
oil for frying
6 oz/175 g Roquefort cheese
12 walnuts
walnut oil and lemon juice to taste
2 lettuce hearts

Cut the crusts off the bread and cut them into tiny squares. Fry quickly in oil until they are golden all over. Drain on a paper towel. Cut the cheese into squares and roughly chop the walnuts. Mix all the ingredients together, toss in walnut oil and lemon juice and serve immediately.

To prepare: 5 minutes

Spinach, Mushroom and Bacon Salad | Serves 4

One of my favourite restaurants in London serves this salad in huge wooden bowls as a main course. I love it so much that I never get around to choosing other things from the menu!

2 lb/900 g fresh young spinach leaves
1 lb/450 g mushrooms
24 slices of bacon
chopped herbs
½ pint/300ml garlic mayonnaise

Wash and drain the spinach. Slice the mushrooms, and fry the bacon until it is very crispy. Arrange in a wooden bowl and sprinkle herbs over the top. Finally spoon the mayonnaise around in a decorative pattern and it is ready to serve.

To prepare: 6 minutes

French Bean Salad   Serves 2

The subtlety of French beans mixed with good oil and salami has a finesse which is the hallmark of a caring cook.

8 oz/225 g French beans
2 fl oz/55 ml good olive oil
salt
1 oz/25 g salami, very thinly sliced

Lightly cook the beans 'al dente'. Drain, and while still warm toss them in olive oil and season to taste with salt. Remove the rind from the salami and cut the slices into thin strips. Mix into the beans and serve with granary bread and unsalted butter as a salad starter, or as a side salad for an omelette.

To prepare: 6 minutes

Blender Fruit Whip
Stuffed Baked Peaches
Plums with Watermelon
Pear Delight
Orange Slices
Melon with Blackberries
Chocolate Pears
Slivered Pineapple
Mandarin Compote
Granny's Apples
Penny's Sorbet
Banana and Apricot Whip
Barbecued Bananas
Baked Bananas
Flaming Peaches
Fresh Fruit and Yogurt
Grilled Grapes
Cream Crunch
Peter's Pudding
Zabaione
Fruit Jelly Cream
Omelette Soufflés
Syllabubs
Florentines
Spiced Iced Coffee

When it comes to a dessert course you may feel that your minutes are running out on you – but be reassured, many of the recipes here can be made without having to think about them at all. If you can stock your freezer with some good quality sorbets and ice cream, so much the better – you will always have an elegant dessert on hand. But in some cases a dessert course may not be essential – many people are delighted with a cheese board or fresh fruit or both, and sometimes I skip straight from the main course to coffee and serve little sweet goodies to round off the meal. An easy way out, yes, but it's a successful one. But for when you do have those minutes to spare, here are some desserts which will be fitting finales to your memorable meals.

Blender Fruit Whip

Serves 4

On paper this looks hideously instant, but actually it makes a beautiful mousse.

1 tablespoon (15 ml spoon) gelatine
juice of half a lemon
½ cup boiling water
2 egg whites
10 oz/275 g canned peaches
2 oz/50 g castor sugar

Put the gelatine, lemon juice and water into the blender and liquidise for 40 seconds. Add the egg whites and blend for 30 seconds longer. Add the fruit and sugar and liquidise until well-mixed. Pour into a bowl or mould and chill for 2 hours.

To prepare: 3 minutes
Chill for 2 hours

Stuffed Baked Peaches

Serves 4

These peaches are worth every moment you spend on them. They make a fine end to an elegant meal.

6 peaches
6 macaroons, crushed
2 oz/50 g flaked almonds
a little icing sugar
1 tablespoon (15 ml spoon) mixed peel
a little sherry

Pre-heat oven to gas mark 4/350°F/180°C

Cut the peaches in half, crush the macaroons, and grill the almonds on both sides for a few minutes until they are browned. Combine the macaroon crumbs with a little sugar and the mixed peel and add to the nuts. Moisten with a little sherry. Fill the peach halves with the mixture and bake uncovered for 30 minutes. Serve warm, with cream.

To prepare: 8 minutes
Cooking time: 30 minutes

Plums with Watermelon

Serves 6

A refreshing way to end a meal: the combination of these two fruits is outstanding.

1 watermelon
8 oz/225 g each plums and greengages
icing sugar to sweeten

Cut the watermelon in half and scoop out the flesh. Discard the seeds. Chop it into little dice, and then halve, stone and chop the plums and greengages. Mix all together, sweeten to taste with sifted icing sugar and pile the fruit high in the half-melon shells. Serve chilled, on crushed ice.

To prepare: 8 minutes

Pear Delight

Serves 4

This recipe delights all ages, hence its name.

4 ripe pears
juice of 1 lemon
3 tablespoons (3 × 15 ml spoons) Kirsch
2 oz/50 g castor sugar
4 portions of vanilla ice cream
2 oz/50 g crushed macaroons
2 oz/50 g toasted flaked almonds

Peel, core and slice the pears (or you can use peaches if you prefer, or a combination of the two). Sprinkle with the lemon juice, Kirsch and sugar, and chill for an hour. Serve with the ice cream and sprinkle with the crumbs and nuts mixed together.

To prepare: 5 minutes
Chill for 1 hour

Orange Slices

This is a classic recipe which I have used for years and adapted to making in a matter of minutes. I never tire of it.

3 medium oranges
3 tablespoons (3 × 15 ml spoons) castor sugar
4 tablespoons (4 × 15 ml spoons) water
2 tablespoons (2 × 15 ml spoons) brandy

Peel and slice the oranges, removing the pith and pips. Make a syrup with the sugar and water by boiling them together for 5 minutes. Cool, add the brandy and pour over the oranges. Chill.

To prepare: 10 minutes
Chill for at least 1 hour

Melon with Blackberries

Serves 4

The alliance of blackberry and melon is sublime, and this is the best dessert I know for the Indian summer days that we so often get in September, the month of blackberries.

1 melon
12 oz/350 g blackberries
4 scoops of vanilla ice cream

Cut the melon in half and scoop out the seeds. Fill each hole with the ripe, sweet blackberries. Serve chilled, topped with a scoop of soft vanilla ice cream.

To prepare: 4 minutes
Chill for 1 hour

Chocolate Pears

Serves 2

This is really Poire Helène gone simple, but it's awfully good.

1 tin of pears
3 oz/75 g good plain chocolate
2 oz/55 ml water
1 oz/25 g sugar
vanilla essence
2 scoops of vanilla ice cream

Put 2 pear halves per person into the bottom of a tall glass. Melt the chocolate with the water in a bowl over a pan of hot water and then add a few drops of vanilla essence. Pour the hot sauce over the pears and serve immediately with a scoop of vanilla ice cream on top.

To prepare: 5 minutes

Slivered Pineapple

Serves 4

My mother's cook in Cambridge was a master of the art of slicing – or shaving is probably a better word – pineapple. He did it so finely and evenly that it seemed incredible that it had been done by human hand. The result was a refined dessert fit to be served to the most distinguished dons in the city – which it was. I advocate practice and a really good, sharp steel knife.

Cut the outer husk off the pineapple and then sliver it as finely and evenly as you possibly can. Lay the slivers in a wide glass dish and sprinkle them with castor sugar, leaving them to make their own juice. Serve chilled, either as it is or with coffee ice cream with which it has a special affinity.

To prepare: 10 minutes
Chill for 1 hour

Mandarin Compote

Serves 4

Although this looks horribly like cheating, the softened apple contributes the unexpected to the canned fruit and it makes a remarkably good fruit dessert.

1 10 oz/275 g tin of mandarin oranges
2 tablespoons (2 × 15 ml spoons) sugar
8 oz/225 g apples
1 glass of water

Add the sugar to the juice from the can and heat gently until dissolved. Peel and core the apples and chop them finely. Heat gently in the syrup until the apple softens, about 4 minutes. Add the mandarin sections and chill.

To prepare: 5 minutes
Chill for 2 hours

Granny's Apples

Serves 6

This variation on the stuffed baked apple elevates it to gastronomic status.

6 Granny Smith apples
4 oz/100 g dates
2 oz/50 g crystallised ginger
2 oz/50 g mixed peel
2 tablespoons (2 × 15 ml spoons) apricot jam
sugar to taste
1 glass white wine
1 small carton double cream

Pre-heat oven to gas mark 4/350°F/180°C

Core the apples and stuff with the chopped dates, sliced ginger and peel mixed with the apricot jam. Stand in an ovenproof dish and pour a little wine and cream over each one. Bake for 25-30 minutes.

To prepare: 6 minutes
Cooking time: 25 minutes

Penny's Sorbet

Serves 6

My friend Penny came to the rescue when I despaired of making my own sorbets – they always separated or crystallised, and I was having a moan. A little while later I was the triumphant creator of a successful sorbet!

1 large tin peaches, with its juices
½ pint/275 ml fresh orange juice
sugar to taste
juice of half a lemon

Liquidise and freeze, stirring after 1 hour in the freezer. Leave for 4 hours to freeze through.

To prepare: 2 minutes
Freeze for a total of 5 hours

Banana and Apricot Whip

Serves 4

Just one minute next to the blender and a delicious pudding is made . . .

1 medium tin of apricots, with its juices
2 bananas
1 small carton double cream, whipped

Liquidise the fruit with the juices and stir in the whipped cream. Chill.

To prepare: 2 minutes

Barbecued Bananas

Believe it or not – and I didn't until recently – you can barbecue bananas in their skins on the dwindling coals as you eat whatever you have cooked over the barbecue fire. Leave them over the heat, turning, until the skins are browned all over. Slit them down the middle and fill them with whipped cream and a dash of brandy. They are fantastic.

Cooking time: whilst you eat your first course

Baked Bananas

For when the weather does not permit barbecuing.

Slice 1 banana per person thickly, sprinkle with lemon juice and brown sugar, and bake them, covered, in a buttered dish for 20 minutes at gas mark 4/350°F/180°C. Serve with cream.

To prepare: 1 minute
Cooking time: 20 minutes

Flaming Peaches   Serves 2

A dinner party piece, this, which takes you away from the table for only a couple of minutes.

4 peaches
1 oz/25 g butter
3 tablespoons (3× 15 ml spoons) brandy
¼ pint/150 ml cream

Skin, stone and slice the peaches and heat through in the butter. Heat the brandy in a little pan, pour over the peach slices and set fire to it. Pour over the cream, stir around and serve immediately.

To prepare: 2 minutes per peach
Cooking time: 2 minutes

Fresh Fruit and Yogurt

This is a light and refreshing dessert, ideal to round off a quick – and of course memorable – lunch. Just choose your fruit – fresh or canned, and in the summer any of the soft fruits are delicious – and mix them with natural yogurt. Serve with a bowl of castor sugar.

To prepare: 2 minutes

Grilled Grapes   Serves 4

For such a simple dish this really qualifies as gastronomic. It also works beautifully with sliced peaches.

1 lb/450 g seedless grapes
½ pint/275 ml double cream
2 tablespoons (2 × 15 ml spoons) soft brown sugar

Put the grapes into a heatproof dish and cover with the whipped cream. Sprinkle with the sugar and place under a hot grill just long enough for the sugar to bubble. Serve at once.

To prepare: 2 minutes
Grilling time: 3-4 minutes

Cream Crunch

Serves 4

Kid's play really – and kids love it so don't let them get near it if it's not for them!

½ pint/275 ml double cream
2 tablespoons (2 × 15 ml) cold coffee
2 Crunchie bars

Whip the cream so that it is fairly stiff. Mix in the cold coffee, break up the Crunchie bars into little pieces and fold in. Serve immediately.

To prepare: 2 minutes

Peter's Pudding

Serves 2

This has a unique sophistication and an unusual beauty. Serve it with stewed Victoria plums.

3 oz/75 g cream cheese
3 tablespoons (3 × 15 ml spoons) marmalade
2 tablespoons (2 × 15 ml spoons) whisky

Mix the ingredients together and freeze.

To prepare: 1 minute
Freeze for 4 hours

Zabaione

This classic Italian dish requires an eagle eye but nothing is more delicious

8 egg yolks
8 tablespoons (8 × 15 ml spoons) icing sugar
4 sherry glasses Marsala

Beat the yolks with the sifted sugar until pale and frothy, and stir in the Marsala. Over a very gentle heat, in a thick pan, stir constantly until it thickens, being very careful not to let it curdle. Pour into glasses and serve immediately.

To prepare: 5 minutes

Fruit Jelly Cream

Serves 2

This is a lovely light dish, and you can add chopped fruit to it if you wish.

2 teaspoons (2 × 5 ml spoons) gelatine
2 tablespoons (2 × 15 ml spoons) hot water
¼ pint/150 ml fruit juice
half a carton of natural yogurt

Dissolve the gelatine in the water over a very low heat and add to the fruit juice. Mix with the yogurt and leave to set. Serve with a bowl of castor sugar.

To prepare: 3 minutes
Chill for 1 hour

Omelette Soufflés

Allow 1 egg per person. Separate the yolks from the whites, then beat the latter until very stiff. Without washing the beater whisk the yolks until they are pale yellow with ½ oz/12 g castor sugar per egg. Mix in a little cream or top of the milk and fold the whites in. Cook in a heavy buttered frying pan until it begins to rise, then put your chosen filling in the middle. Fold over and cook through, being careful that the bottom of the omelette does not burn. Serve immediately, dusted with sifted icing sugar.

To prepare: 5 minutes

Some Fillings
halved grapes and grated apple
raspberries sweetened with honey
pears in chocolate sauce
chopped apple and ginger
sliced oranges
jam

Syllabubs
Serves 2

This most stylish and exquisite of old-fashioned desserts makes a marvellous party piece.

1 small glass of sherry
2 tablespoons (2 × 15 ml spoons) brandy
1 lemon or orange
2 oz/50 g castor sugar
½ pint/275 ml double cream
grated nutmeg

Combine the sherry and the brandy and soak the peel of the orange or lemon in it for several hours or overnight. Strain and add the sugar, and stir until it dissolves. Add the cream gradually, stirring constantly. Grate a little nutmeg into the cream, and then whisk it until it thickens, being careful not to overdo it otherwise the mixture will stiffen and curdle. Spoon the syllabub into glasses and chill.

To prepare: 5 minutes
Soak the peel for a minimum of 2 hours
Chill for 2 hours

COFFEE TIME

And now for the coffee course. I am very fond of serving little goodies with the coffee instead of a dessert – an easy way out but one which a lot of people seem to like. Halva, the scrumptious sinful Greek sweetmeat, is a great favourite, and chocolates never fail. Nor do these:

Florentines

Makes 18

2 oz/50 g castor sugar
2 oz/50 g flaked almonds
1 tablespoon (15 ml spoon) plain flour
1½ oz/40 g butter
1 tablespoon (15 ml spoon) single cream

Pre-heat oven to gas mark 4/350°F/180°C

Put these ingredients into a saucepan and heat gently, stirring until blended. Do not overheat. Add 2 oz/50 g finely sliced glacé cherries and heap teaspoons of the mixture on to rice paper in a baking tray. Bake for 10 minutes and cool on a rack.

To prepare: 4 minutes
Cooking time: 10 minutes

Spiced Iced Coffee

Serves 1

If you want to combine dessert and coffee all in one, try this recipe – it is decadent but delicious.

1 cup double-strength coffee
a little pared orange peel
1 scoop vanilla ice cream
a little whipped cream
grated nutmeg
1 cinnamon stick

Put the peel into the coffee and let it cool a little. Put the ice cream into each cup of coffee and top with the whipped cream. Sprinkle with grated nutmeg and stir with the cinnamon stick!

SOME BASIC RECIPES

Garlic Butter

2 oz/50 g salted butter
1 large clove of garlic, peeled
chopped fresh parsley (optional)

Melt the butter in a pan over a gentle heat and add the crushed
garlic. Stir for a few minutes and then add the parsley if required.
Chill in the refrigerator.

Tarragon Butter

Chop a small bunch of fresh tarragon very finely and mix into 2 oz/
50 g melted butter.

Vinaigrette

1 tablespoon (15 ml spoon) vinegar
1 teaspoon (5 ml spoon) mustard
salt and pepper
optional garlic
¼ pint/150 ml olive oil

Mix the vinegar and the mustard in a small bowl and season with salt
and pepper. Add crushed garlic to taste if required. Add the olive oil
gradually, stirring all the time until the vinaigrette begins to thicken.
Leave to stand for a while before using so that the flavours permeate
the oil.

Mayonnaise

2 egg yolks
1 teaspoon (5 ml spoon) dry mustard
salt and pepper
½ pint/275 ml olive oil

Put the egg yolks into the blender and add the mustard, salt and pepper. Liquidise, and then through the hole in the top of the lid pour a thin stream of oil on to the eggs with the machine running. Stop pouring from time to time to let the mixture thicken. When the oil is all used up and the mayonnaise a good consistency, pour into a screw-top jar and refrigerater. It will keep for a week or two.

INDEX

MORE COOKERY BOOKS FROM CORONET

DELIA SMITH

☐	16876 5	How To Cheat At Cooking	£1.50
☐	21002 8	Frugal Food	£1.50
☐	23094 0	Evening Standard Cookbook	£1.50
☐	22158 5	Book of Cakes	£1.50

PRIYA WICKRAMASINGHE

☐	26676 7	Spicy and Delicious	£1.40

DEANNA BROSTOFF

☐	28755 1	Cooking For One And Two	£1.50

CAROLINE LIDDELL

☐	25454 8	The Wholefoods Cookbook	£1.50

All these books are available at your local bookshop or newsagent, or can be ordered direct from the publisher. Just tick the titles you want and fill in the form below.

Prices and availability subject to change without notice.

KNIGHT BOOKS, P.O. Box 11, Falmouth, Cornwall.
Please send cheque or postal order, and allow the following for postage and packing:

U.K.– 45p for one book, plus 20p for the second book, and 14p for each additional book ordered up to a £1.63 maximum.

B.F.P.O. and **Eire** – 45p for the first book, plus 20p for the second book, and 14p per copy for the next 7 books, 8p per book thereafter.

OTHER OVERSEAS CUSTOMERS – 75p for the first book, plus 21p per copy for each additional book.

Name ....

Address ....

....